VLADIMIR NABOKOV:
The Velvet Butterfly

by
Alan Levy

THE PERMANENT PRESS
Sag Harbor, New York 11963

copyright© 1984 by Alan Levy

Part 1 of this book appeared, in a shorter form, in <u>The New York Times Magazine</u> of October 31, 1971.

Photos copyright© 1984 by Horst Tappe, A.S.M.P. All rights reserved.

Library of Congress number: 83-063247
International Standard Book Number: 0-932966-41-1

Excerpts from THE REAL LIFE OF SEBASTIAN KNIGHT, by Vladimer Nabokov, © 1941, 1959 by New Directions Publishing Corporation, reprinted with permission.

Excerpt from PNIN by Vladimir Nabokov. Copyright© 1953, 1954, 1955, 1957 by Vladimir Nabokov. Reprinted by permission of Doubleday & Company, Inc.

Excerpts from PROSPERO'S PROGRESS, from "I HAVE NEVER SEEN A MORE LUCID, MORE LONELY, BETTER BALANCED MAD MIND THAN MINE" by Vladimir Nabokov, reprinted by permission from TIME.

Excerpts from SPEAK, MEMORY reprinted by permission of Article 3B Literary Trust of Vladimir Nabokov, Vera Nabokov Trustee.

Copyrighted excerpts from ADA, from KING, QUEEN, KNAVE, from LOOK AT THE HARLEQUINS!, from MARY, from GLORY, from TRANSPARENT THINGS, by Vladimir Nabokov, and from THE ANNOTATED LOLITA, by Alfred Appel, Jr., reprinted with permission of McGraw-Hill Book Company.

Reprinted by permission of G.P. Putnam's Sons from PALE FIRE by Vladimir Nabokov. Copyright© 1962 by G.P. Putnam's Sons.

Reprinted by permission of G.P. Putnam's Sons from DESPAIR by Vladimir Nabokov. Copyright© 1965, 1966 by Vladimir Nabokov.

Reprinted by permission of G.P. Putnam's Sons from LOLITA by Vladimir Nabokov. Copyright© 1955 by Vladimir Nabokov.

Reprinted by permission of G.P. Putnam's Sons from THE GIFT by Vladimir Nabokov. Copyright© 1963 by G.P. Putnam's Sons.

Reprinted by permission of G.P. Putnam's Sons from THE DEFENSE by Vladimir Nabokov. Copyright© 1964 by Vladimir Nabokov.

Reprinted by permission of G.P. Putnam's Sons from INVITATION TO A BEHEADING by Vladimir Nabokov. Copyright© 1959 by Vladimir Nabokov.

THE PERMANENT PRESS, Noyac Road, Sag Harbor, New York, 11963.
Printed in the United States of America.

A PREFACE TO THE FIRST THREE PORTRAIT BOOKS

When my profiles-in-depth of W. H. Auden, Vladimir Nabokov, and Ezra Pound first appeared in the New York Times Magazine in the early 1970's, I received many letters and a few transatlantic calls from editors and publishers who all voiced the same regret: that these articles must die the natural deaths of yesterday's paper or last week's Sunday supplement.

Their solutions, no matter how winningly phrased did not grab me —for I had heard their gists and piths before. Basically, these proposals boiled down to two. The Vertical Approach: "Why don't you paste them up, together with some others you've done, and we'll publish a collection?" To which my response was: "For whom?"... The Horizontal Approach: "How about expanding this one [or that one] into a definitive biography?" The answer came particularly easily in Pound's case: "It took me two weeks to get two hundred words of quotes from him, so I don't think I'll live long enough to do a full-length biography." At the time, Pound was eighty-six and I was thirty-nine.

I also recognized that, from each of the three writers, I had drawn all or almost all that personal contact was going to elicit. And yet I wasn't ready to let go of them.

The solution dawned when one editor, Howard Greenfeld, began by reminding me: "These are all old men. For one or more of them, this may be the last public appearance before the obituary notices." Howard went on to stress my obligation to students and others who were just starting to discover and read these authors: to put my work, their output, and their lives into some solid, useful order.

I realized that, when I had been an undergraduate at Brown University and a graduate student at Columbia, and just starting to read Pound and Auden (Nabokov was still "too new" then), I certainly would have welcomed an informed introduction to them as living men rather than assigned authors.

Howard Greenfeld being an American editor living in Europe in the next country to mine, he and I were able to continue the discussion over many months — and out of it has come this small cottage industry of PORTRAIT BOOKS: published for library, critical, gift-giving, student, and general use. These first three are — and the Portrait Books to come in future years will be — works of enthusiastic journalistic scholarship researched and written, firsthand, by one man who knew his subjects well and intensely . . . who read everything by them . . . and who likes and cares for what he is writing about. These books have a uniform format — though the lengths and styles of the components can be as different as Nabokov is from Pound is from Auden.

Part 1. THE MAN: A biographical portrait, drawn from my initial magazine interviews. They are never padded, though sometimes they are fleshed out with material that was omitted or lost to the magazine's editorial, puritanical, or space needs. Nor are the magazine profiles drastically reworked, except to fit the needs of each book and bring it up-to-date. All of the first three heroes have died in the interim between article and book, but each first chapter remains a meeting with the living man in the context of his living word.

Part 2. QUOTES: A mosaic of words by and about the man you've just met. This section is organized with an ear to the rhythm as well as the flavor of whatever he has done to merit your attention.

Part 3. An essay on EXPERIENCING him, not just reading him or reading about him. Written conversationally, this is a verbal map, with a few guidelines, for a voyage of discovery in which you share some of What It's Like and How It Feels to be reading Nabokov or Auden or Pound, hearing him on records, and perhaps attending his plays or movies. It is narrated with my own personal insights and affection for the works. I must emphasize that this is NOT a critical essay. At my most waspish, I may warn you off a redundant lesser work or vent my outrage at the kind of critical study that erects barriers of boredom and trivia between you and the artist, of which Goodman's *Tragedy of Sebastian Knight* is a classic example — so I never want to feel guilty of the same crime against literature. And this chapter should be read NOT as a substitute for actually experiencing the artist, but as an appetizer or as a companion to the essential experience.

Part 4. A comprehensive BIBLIOGRAPHY that does what most bibliographies I've seen don't do: it takes cognizance of paperback and hardcover reissues, instead of merely listing all the relevant details of the original 1910 or 1967 edition, now out of print, by a publisher who is now out of business. And it contains Library of Congress catalog listings as well as Dewey decimal shelf numbers. This will tell you where to look in your own library's alphabetical card file and may even enable you to go directly to the specific shelf where you'll find a certain book or related works. In this effort, I was blessed in the 1970s by the heroic labors of Joseph H. Podoski of Washington, D.C., a retired Librarian of Congress and in the 1980s with the assistance of my daughter Monica and my wife Valerie on visits to the Library of Congress. Special thanks are due to graphic artist Norman Merems of Vienna for streamlining what otherwise would have been a particularly dense and cumbersome Nabokov bibliography. A special feature of the Nabokov bibliography is that it contains call numbers and other details of Russian versions available from Ardis Books or in the Library of Congress Slavic division or Rare Book collection.

Part 5: A simple factual CHRONOLOGY of the man's life and career for compact easy reference. For this common-sense suggestion, I am grateful to Prof. Alden Todd (author of *Finding Facts Fast*), who had the common sense to suggest it.

These books are illustrated — partly with archive shots and most notably with photos by the man I consider the best portrait photographer working in Europe today: Horst Tappe of Montreux, Switzerland. A photographer of rare cultural and personal sensitivity as well as talent, Horst has often been the key who opened the doors to my audiences with great men.

Ezra Pound died in 1972, W. H. Auden in 1973, and Vladimir Nabokov in 1977. All three of them long ago earned their immortality, but it is my hope that these small books of mine will ease the path for your understanding and enjoyment of WHY they will live on.

ALAN LEVY PORTRAIT BOOKS:
1. EZRA POUND: The Voice of Silence
2. W. H. AUDEN: In the Autumn of the Age of Anxiety
3. VLADIMIR NABOKOV: The Velvet Butterfly

Dedication:
To
CELIA SAGNOUS
and
ESTHER LEVY,
*eternal sisters
and
grand aunts*

CONTENTS

A Preface to the First Three Portrait Books   *iii*
Part 1: The Man: Nabokov-Hunting in the Alps   1
Part 2: "Invent the World! Invent Reality!":
          A Portrait in Quotes
Part 3: Experiencing Vladimir Nabokov   1
Part 4: Bibliography: "The Palliative of Articulate Art"
Part 5: Chronology: 1899 to 1977

1
THE MAN:
NABOKOV-HUNTING IN THE ALPS

"From the age of seven . . . my first glance of the morning was for the sun, my first thought was for the butterflies it would engender . . . I have hunted butterflies in various climes and disguises: as a pretty boy in knickerbockers and sailor cap; as a lanky cosmospolitan expatriate in flannel bags and beret; as a fat hatless old man in shorts." —Vladimir Nabokov in his autobiography, *Speak, Memory.*

MONTREUX, SWITZERLAND 1971

In the glassed-in greenhouse that lobbies for the Edwardian rococo Montreux-Palace Hotel, a dozen Trumanesque tourists and their plum-pudding ladies are worrying each other about the weather—asking anxiously whether the weather will hold for their air-conditioned sightseeing excursion. Right in their midst, but clearly not part of them, a professorial old gent is exulting: "It's been a wonderful summer for butterflies! Generally, their emergences are staggered. But this year, May and June were such bad months that the butterflies just waited—and then they all came out together!"

His enthusiasm cuts through the querulousness around him—and strangers eavesdrop. (Younger voyeurs have even sneaked photos of him while he was relaxing beside the hotel's pool.) The most distinguished permanent resident of the Montreux-Palace, Vladimir Nabokov stands out in that crowd of transients not only because, well into his seventies, he's slightly older yet much spryer than the Tour, but also because he dresses more like a tourist than the tourists: windbreaker over gold button-down sport shirt tucked into gray pin-striped shorts meshing with sun-textured freckled knees. Add to all this the gold-handled butterfly net (from an "entomological instruments store on Thirty-third Street") in his right hand, and the net effect is septuagenarian Hulot—stooped a little by age, but the better to lean into the butterfly hunt that is looming. Now Hulot dons a white cap—and, *voilà,* instant Magoo!

The old magician tells stories, too, in a hale and hearty hiker's voice. My admiration for his "entomological instrument" elicits

1

the tale of a lavishly-equipped, heavily-laden, and baggily-dressed photographer who descended upon the author of *Lolita* and *Ada:* "I was curious about all the technology he carried, so he opened up his fancy camera case for me and there was his trouser belt! 'I've been looking for it all morning,' the man said putting it on right then and there."

"Freud would have a field day with that," I remark. Nabokov can be expected to snap at the bait, for he has penned and punned so vehemently and so often against "the Viennese witch-doctor," "quack," and "charlatan"; "Freudian voodooism"; "the lewd, ludicrous, and vulgar . . . Signy-Mondieu analysts"; and (even in his autobiography!) "a huge custard-colored balloon . . . inflated by Sigismond Lejoyeux, a local aeronaut." He has written: "I reject completely the vulgar, shabby, fundamentally medieval world of Freud with its crankish quest for sexual symbols (something like searching for Baconian acrostics in Shakespeare's works) and its bitter little embryos spying from their natural nooks upon the love life of their parents." And he has said: "I don't want an elderly gentleman with an umbrella inflicting his dreams upon me. *I* don't have the dreams that he discusses in his books. I don't see umbrellas in my dreams. Or balloons."

Having vented his contempt in print (where one recognizes that it is based on a thorough familiarity with Freud), Nabokov can now afford to be benign in conversation. "A Freudian can have a field day with an object at hand" is how he parries my thrust—and, to demonstrate, here in the public rooms of the Montreux-Palace, Nabokov deftly manipulates his butterfly net like an outstretched umbrella—and it suddenly balloons to its maximum erection of thirty-six inches.

He does this with such animal dexterity that one of the Bess Truman ladies giggles, gasps, clucks, and asks: "Who *is* that man? He's not one of *us,* is he?

The Soviet Union's *Short Literary Encyclopedia* (vol. V, 1968) answers the lady's question rather objectively—so objectively, in fact, that the whole volume has been officially attacked for "objectivism":

> Vladimir Vladimirovich Nabokov (1899-   )
> —Russian-American writer. Son of V. D. Nabokov, a leader of the Kadet Party. Finished the Tenishev School. Published his first collection of poetry in 1916. From 1919

he has been in emigration, where in 1922 he finished Trinity College (Cambridge). He achieved literary recognition after the publication of the novel *Mary* in 1926. N's works bear an extremely contradictory character. Among his most interesting works are the ... long story *The Defense* (1929-30), which depicts the life tragedy of a phenomenal chess player, the novels *Laughter in the Dark* (1932-3), *Despair* (1934 . . .), the stories ... which reflect the process of spiritual bestialization of the bourgeoisie in Germany as it was becoming Fascist. In the novel *The Gift* (1937 . . .) N. presents a tendentiously distorted picture of N.G. Chernyshevsky. N.'s books are characterized by literary snobbism, replete with literary reminiscences. His style is marked by excessively refined "estrangement" of devices and the frequent use of mystification. These same features are also characteristic of his lyrics. In N.'s prose the influence of F. Kafka and M. Proust can be felt; such is the novel *Invitation to a Beheading* (1935-6. . .) in which N. describes the nightmarish existence of a little man surrounded by the monstrous phantasma of the contemporary world. Such are the features which made possible the "denationalization" of the work of N.—who in 1940 began to write in English. Since that time he has lived in the USA where for some time he taught literature in universities. Among his books of this period are . . . the erotic best-seller *Lolita* (1955), the novel *Pnin* (1957). He translates Russian classical poetry into English. In 1964 he published a translation of A. S. Pushkin's *Eugene Onegin* in four volumes with extensive commentaries.

    Aside from overlooking Nabokov's return to Europe in 1960 and his consummate masterpiece, *Pale Fire* (which will share a pedestal here with *Lolita*), this Soviet listing is more complete than many *Who's Who*s. But his Russian chronologers take no note of his acclaim by serious critics as "America's greatest literary glory" (Anthony Burgess) and our "best living American Writer" (John Updike) and the "most original writer and stylist since Joyce" (*Time* Magazine); nor do they credit their fellow Slav with adding the improper nouns *"nymphet"* and *"lolita"* to the English language. And, for all their objectivism, they could never begin to depict the *Hotelmensch* whose adult life has been spent camping in motels, cabins, furnished flats, sublet homes of professors on sabbaticals (moving from year to year, sometimes from term to term) ... who calls the Montreux-Palace "a rosy and optimistic place for an exile" ... and who has never owned a home because "nothing short of a replica of my childhood surroundings would have satisfied me. I would never manage to match my memories correctly—so why trouble with hopeless approximations."

VlaDEEmear NahBUCKof, sometimes incorrectly called NABohkov, NabOkov, NahboKOV, Nahbacocoa, NaBOREkopf, etc. *("One cannot hope to understand an author if one cannot even pronounce his name"),* is a man with "no country but himself. He is the only refugee who could have turned statelessness into absolute strength," says Alfred Kazin. Serialized in *Playboy* and *The New Yorker* and Covered by *Time,* Nabokov was proclaimed by *Time* in 1969 as "an exile, a man who has triumphantly survived this century of the refugee, a man who has lost everything, yet transformed his losses through art and levity into a habitation of the mind."

Once upon a time, quoting Nabokov to Nabokov, I wrote to him:

"You say [at the end of *Pale Fire*]: 'I may turn up yet, on another campus, as an old, happy, healthy, heterosexual Russian, a writer in exile, sans fame, sans future, sans audience, sans anything but his art ... Oh, I may do many things! History permitting, I may sail back to my recovered kingdom, and with a great sob greet the gray coastline and the gleam of a roof in the rain. I may huddle and groan in a madhouse ...' I haven't read *Speak, Memory* yet, but I will have by the time we next meet. When did you realize that you weren't going back to your native land in the near or distant future?"

Nabokov, I knew, prefers to handle the most serious and delicate questions (more recently, *ALL* questions) in writing. When five single-spaced pages of *Q&A*s came back to me in the mail, I found that, among all my questions, he had evaded this one by altering it to:

> Q: In *Speak, Memory,* which I have now read, you, and memory, speak of your non-Russian lineage. Could you climb that side of the family tree a little higher?
>
> A: On the side of my paternal grandmother who was born Baroness von Korff, there are the von Korffs, traceable to the Fourteenth century, and on their distaff side a long line of von Tiesenhausen of Livland, who took part, around 1200, in the Third and Fourth Crusades. Another direct ancestor of mine, was Can Grande della Scala, Prince of Verona, who sheltered the exiled Dante Alighieri and whose blazon (two big dogs holding a ladder) adorns Boccaccio's *Decameron* (1353). Della Scala's granddaughter Beatrice married in 1370 Wilhelm, Count Oettingen, grandson of Bolko III, Duke of Silesia. Their daughter married a von Waldburg, and three Waldburgs, one Kittlitz, two Polenzs, and ten Osten-Sackens later, Wilhelm Carl von Korff and his wife, Eleonor von der Osten-Sacken engendered my paternal grandmother's grandfather Nikolaus, killed in battle on June 12, 1812. I have some more of those barons up my sleeve but that will do for the moment.

Thus copes Nabokov with past removed and past denied. Further literary detection revealed only that, living in Berlin in 1927, Nabokov was still "absolutely sure, with a number of other intelligent people, that sometime in the next decade, we would all be back in a hospitable, remorseful, racemosa-blooming Russia." But, with "the passing of years, I grew less and less interested in Russia and more and more indifferent to the once-harrowing thought that my books would remain banned there as long as my contempt for the police state and political oppression prevented me from entertaining the vaguest thought of return."

Through the late fifties and sixties, while the Soviets were revising and rewriting *their* history, Nabokov was busily translating and co-translating (often with his only child, opera singer Dmitri) and revising his earlier works from their original Russian. In his preface to 1966's English rendition of 1931's *Despair*, he wrote:

> The ecstatic love of a young writer for the old writer he will be some day is ambition in its most laudable form. This love is not reciprocated by the older man in his larger library, for even if he does recall with regret a naked palate and rheumless eye, he has nothing but an impatient shrug for the bungling apprentice of his youth.

No loss of ardor and no witty deceits have mellowed Nabokov's lifelong love for butterflies—a passion that has granted him immortality as discoverer of finds that "will dwell, in generations more numerous than editions." Some of his discoveries have been named after him—and his memory speaks with rapture of "that blessed black night in the Wasatch Range" when he boxed one of them, now classified as Nabokov's Pug [Eupithecia *nabokovi* McDunnough] "on a picture window of James Laughlin's Alta Lodge in Utah" in 1943.*

From 1942 to 1948, while lecturing on literature at Wellesley, Nabokov was also a Harvard Research Fellow in lepidoptera at the Museum of Comparative Zoology. Toward the end of any Nabokov novel, when its artistic "cycle" is complete, a butterfly or moth will make a fleeting, incidental appearance. In *King Queen Knave*, it is perchance "a famous young man who flitted all summer from resort to resort like a velvet butterfly." "To know Nabokov at his best," a mutual friend told me, "is to know him when he's with butterflies." And thus was decreed the summit of my brief friendship with the inventor of Humbert Humbert and Van Veen, Dolores Haze and Clare Quilty, Timofey Pnin and Cincinnatus C. and Vivian Darkbloom, who once wrote under a pseudonym:

> And the highest enjoyment of timelessness—
> in a landscape selected at random—is when
> I stand among rare butterflies and their food
> plants. This is ecstasy, and behind the ecstasy

---

*James Laughlin of New Directions was Nabokov's first consistent American publisher.

is something else, which is hard to explain. It is like a momentary vacuum into which rushes all that I love. A sense of oneness with sun and stone. A thrill of gratitude to whom it may concern—to the contrapuntal genius of human fate or to tender ghosts humoring a lucky mortal.

PRAGUE, CZECHOSLOVAKIA

—not the Ardors and Arbors or Ardis—is where this elusive friendship of ours began, a little before we met, though its principal parts were staged in a dream-bright Switzerland. And Prague, stony and brooding, is where Nabokov's aristocratic mother lived in the 1930's on a small pension from the Czechoslovak government and where she died on the eve of World War II.

> ... Prague means little to me, a bleak bridge across a bleak river, rain, the wet gargoyles of some place of worship, a local lepidopterist in an entomological laboratory, growling (in 1923) "Our Germans are bad enough, but our Jews are worse." And the supper à la fourchette, to which Kramarzh, married to a Russian, invited White Russians, and my sister Elena poking casually at an untouched dish and remarking "Oh it's not cream, it's some sort of *chaud-froid*" and being at once swept aside, fork in hand, by a pack of hungry convives ...

(Karel Kramarzh, 1860-1937, was the first premier of the newly-created Czechoslovak nation, 1918-1919, and then, by the time Nabokov knew him, a rightist minority politician opposed to the liberal centrist policies of President Thomas G. Masaryk. *Chaud-froid* is a cooked fowl or game dish served cold with jelly, aspic, or a sauce.)

Toward the end of my own stay (1967-1971) as a correspondent in the Soviet-occupied capital of Czechoslovakia, I started hearing from a middle-aged Czech lady who worked for the Trade Unions' publishing house. She had met me just twice at parties—but now she phoned me sporadically to ask such bizarre questions as: "What means in English when you say *'putty-buff-and-snuff'*? ... or *'engorged heart'*? ... or *'the Mystery of the Menarche'* ?"

She had been entrusted with the task—both enviable and unenviable—of translating *Lolita* into Czech. While Nabokov is banned in his native Russia, his classic is known and even tolerated in some of the Soviet satellites. The woman was working under a contract signed prior to August, 1968's Red Army invasion of Czechoslovakia. While her project was sometimes on and sometimes off the scheduling lists ("It would be better," one of her newer bosses told me, "if this *Lolita* were about a worker"), she was plowing forward steadily but quietly on the Nabokovian assumption that, if nothing else, art will outlive politics.

In October of 1970, when she called me with her latest list of queries, I told her: "Look, I'll be in Montreux interviewing Noel Coward and staying at the hotel where the Nabokovs live. I don't want to impose upon him, but if you'll write him a letter — telling him when I'll be there—he can get in touch with me if he wants to."

MONTREUX 1970

The tweedy host who invited me down to the Green Room for an 11:00 A.M. drink of "coffee-tea-or-grappa" (he opted for the Italian grape brandy) was charming and marvelously self-preserved: even the red veins in his face seemed to glow. He took care of business right away by running down the Prague woman's list:

"Tell her that 'ululate' is not a dirty word . . . 'Lull' is a boy's name; at least, the only person I knew named Lull was a boy . . . 'matted eyelash' means just that—not a pubic hair . . . and a 'red autumn leaf' is a 'red autumn leaf' is a 'red autumn leaf,' not a deflowered nymphet . . ."

Within ten minutes, Nabokov had given me an incisive analysis of *Lolita* which, for all the translator's quibbles and technicalities in her quest for perfection, cut through the critical cant and prurient scholarship that has managed to intrude upon the enjoyment by millions of the "little girl" who keeps Nabokov:

> Q: "After Olympia Press in Paris published *Lolita*, an American critic suggested that *Lolita* was the record of my love affair with the romantic novel. The substitution English language for romantic novel would make this elegant formula more correct."
> Could you elaborate on the nature of

Nabokov and Alan Levy

>   this love affair and tell of its present status as well as its progress since these words were written in 1956?
>
> A: It is now a kind of second marriage, I bald and benevolent, she, difficult but still chic, and much courted. Metaphors apart, I feel a certain hardening of my vocabulary, with London's modish phrases and New England slang no longer oxygenating the blood stream of my style. In a sense, the same thing occurred in regard to my Russian after several years of expatriation in Berlin and Paris.

Having dissected *Lolita* and put her together intact for export to Prague, Vladimir Nabokov relaxed—and chatted about himself, his health, and hotel-living. His health was self-evident. I had already met Nabokov's uphill neighbor, Noel Coward, who lived in Les Avants sur Montreux. Sir Noël, eight months Nabokov's junior, was looking a good eight years older. (He died in 1973.)

Speaking of Coward, whom he'd never met, Nabokov was amused to be living in a community of Humbert Humberts. Coward had been offered the part in Stanley Kubrick's 1962 film of *Lolita* (for which Nabokov wrote a screenplay and the innovative Kubrick used just enough of it to justify Nabokov's legal position as author of the script; Nabokov intends eventually to publish *his* screenplay and Hollywood notes). Coward declined the part of Humbert because (as he put it to me) "we weren't able to finish reading the book." James Mason, who did play the part, lives five miles from Montreux, is a good friend of Nabokov's, and was of Coward's, too. Nabokov did not number himself among the local Humberts.

> Q: "... my creature Humbert is a foreigner and an anarchist, and there are many things, besides nymphets, in which I disagree with him."
>
>   Could you tell me any instances of mistaken identity involving Humbert-and-you as well as the most salient features you and he have in common?
>
> A: Well, we both like tennis.

(Nabokov, indeed, supported himself in Berlin by teaching tennis— and English and Russian as well as authoring crossword puzzles and chess problems.)

Now we talked about a mutual ex-publisher in another country and Nabokov said of him: "He's a rather astute man with a coarse streak right down the middle and—do you know?—I think it's his coarse part that kept me with him for so long. Each time I visited his city, he would take me home for dinner and—every single time! —he would tell me, as we crossed his threshold, that 'This is the house Lolita built.' Well, I've wrecked some lives in my time, but I also like to think that at least I made a house."

As he spoke, we were joined by a tall, regal, alabaster-skinned lady whom Nabokov introduced proudly as "the person to whom I've been married for forty-five years." Véra Evseevna Slonim Nabokov—daughter of a Jewish industrialist from St. Petersburg — is the "To Véra" to whom all of his novels (eight American and nine translated from Russian) published in English are dedicated. She is his confidante, proofreader, stenographer, (his answers to my queries were typed by her), chief literary counselor, and devoted audience —as well a his partner at chess, Scrabble (often played in Russian), hiking, strolling, butterfly-hunting, and business-negotiating. "In wheeling and dealing," says a friend, "he is the silent partner. She does the arguing and he does the deciding."

From their émigré days together in Berlin (1925-1937) and then Paris (1937-1940) through academic days at Wellesley and then Cornell (1948-1959) and onward and upward into Alpine opulence, Mrs. Nabokov has always been the household manager and chauffeur. Despite his Humbert's climactic odyssey through the neon highways and motel courts of America, Nabokov does not pretend to be a driver. Much of *Lolita* was scrawled on index cards in a 1952 Buick during a transcontinental butterfly hunt with Vera at the wheel. Her husband was no help to her at all; he admitted cheerfully to *Time* in 1969: "There are people who can refold maps, too, but I am not one of them" (thereby echoing the line in his incestuous best-selling fiction, *Ada*, published a few weeks ahead of *Time*: "There are people who can fold a road map. Not this writer.")

Because his Véra is fiercely protective of her man, outsiders tend to have more contact with her than with him. Thus, there were those in Montreux who were willing to "assure" me that *she* ghost-writes *him*. "At the very least," said one such confidant, "they certainly must have collaborated on *Invitation to a Beheading.*" They know M. Nabokov as the benign pedestrian who makes a point of buying *Time* and *Newsweek* and the *International Herald Tribune* at three different newsstands because "they're all good shops. It wouldn't be fair to give one of them all the business, would it?"

Q: There is an ugly rumor afoot in Greater Montreux that "Mrs. Nabokov ghost-writes Mr. Nabokov or, at the very least, they collaborate." Could you dignify this with comment as well as some analysis of how such a rumor could get started—particularly among local tradesmen?

A: The charm of that rumor is enhanced by the fact that what most Montreusians seem to know of my work, or of its shadow, is the film *Lolita* (shown in Switzerland half-a-dozen of years ago). My wife reads my stuff only after I have completed the fair copy in long hand on lined index cards which I fill out while standing at my lectern or lolling in the garden. I am an uncommunicative toiler, and in the case of the longer novels my patient first reader awaits the unknown book with serenity for years and years. Formerly, that is before we could afford secretaries, she used to type all my works and correspondence. She continues to read, very carefully, typescripts and proofs, correcting my grotesque misspellings and sometimes querying an obscure or repititious word. She also types my Russian letters. It may very well be that the observant and intelligent people who bring me fruit and wine, or come to repair radiators and radios jump to wrong conclusions because they never see *me* sitting at a desk, let alone typing.

At first meeting, one is most struck by Mrs. Nabokov's crowning glory of snow-white hair. (I still think of her hair whenever I hear the phrase 'White Russian,' " says a former Cornell student of her husband's.) Mrs. Nabokov intercepted my admiration before I could express it in words and she said matter-of-factly: "It started turning when I was twenty-five."

Her husband added: "Véra was a pale blonde when I met her, but it didn't take me long to turn her hair white."

She apologized for joining us a little late, but she had been upstairs searching for two trophies. Now she gave them to me to give to the translator in Prague. One was *Lolita* translated by the author into his native Russian and published in Manhattan—"not because I wanted tourists to smuggle it in, but because I was more afraid some Moscow hack would do a translation and—well—for example, there's no such term as 'blue jeans' in the Russian language."

"I think there is now," I told Nabokov, who hasn't been back to Russia since fleeing the Bolsheviks, more than half a century ago, with his family on a small and shoddy Greek ship *Nadezhda* ("Hope") carrying a cargo of dried fruit. "Behind the Iron Curtain these days, everyone wears one kind of blue jeans—made in East Germany, I think—with the brand-name Super Rifle, in English, sewn indelibly onto the right rear cheek."

Vladimir Nabokov loved that! He repeated it to his wife, who'd been coping with an Italian waiter (who wanted Mr., not Mrs., Nabokov to "autograph the bill," perhaps as a collector's item), and then he began to cackle—at the thought, he explained half a minute later, of some specialist hack going through *Lolita* substituting "Super Rifle" for "blue jeans" every time they appeared: "It would be a whole new book!" By Freud, no doubt.

The Slavonic in his Russian *Lolita* (which retails on the Leningrad black market for twenty rubles, or two *Zhivago*s) would help his Czech translator with her work, he said. The Nabokovs' other trophy for me to take back to her was a huge trade paperback called *The Annotated Lolita*, edited by Professor Alfred Appel, Jr., of Northwestern University. Whereupon, in an outburst of hyperbole that would live on to haunt us, Nabokov described Appel to me as "*my* pedant. A pedant straight out of *Pale Fire*. Every writer should have such a pedant. He was a student of mine at Cornell and later he married a girl I'd taught at another time—and I understand that I was their first shared passion."

Looking positively cherubic, Nabokov paraphrased his earlier remark about wrecking some lives—but making others.

Q: "Nabokov is considered a deadly serious

Vera and Vladimir

cosmic joker. He loves to tell you something which isn't true and have you believe it; but even more he loves to tell you something which is true and make you think he is lying."
—*Celebrity Register* (Cleveland Amory, editor; 1963)
Do you subscribe to this analysis and can you give examples, pro or con? Once, in talking about Mr. and Mrs. Alfred Appel having you in common, you alluded to wrecking lives and building others. Can you elaborate on that?

A: I do not possess that Register, and do not know who said that, but whoever did (here comes a bit of palmistry) is a touchy and basically naive person who writes good English, likes to generalize, and constantly misconstrues another's motives in specific cases of human behavior. I have as many faults as the crust of a mountain chain but deceiving the naive is not one of them. As to your other point, I cannot allude in any detail to the lives which *Lolita* (for example) wrecked, for the people involved are still around; but I can say that those lives were so precariously poised that even *Portnoy's Love Story* would have caused them to topple. (Printer, do not unpun me)

Nabokov spends most of the year—except for business trips and one long butterfly-collecting expedition—in Montreux. The Palace Hotel, he said, provides adequate insulation, but enough uninvited callers still filter through. Some are doing Ph.D. dissertations on him or on a paragraph of his work; others are just admirers or social butterflies or would-be interviewers.

"Every Englishman, no matter what his title or credentials, turns out to be a journalist of some sort—but I enjoy talking with them. The Americans I seem to meet are often out to get more than they're here to give—so I tend to be wary. Not long ago, there was someone with an American name who kept leaving vague messages for me all over Montreux. I started leaving messages, too, that I was unavailable. Then I got one more message—a slip of paper that said 'Fuck you.'

"Well, this was so much more explicit than the others that I asked the desk what kind of person had left this message. And the desk said: 'That wasn't a person, sir; that was two rather wild-looking American girls.' This intrigued me even more—so I looked at the slip of paper again. And there I found something at the end of the message which I hadn't noticed in my first reading: a question mark!"

Mrs. Nabokov changed the subject even before our laughter died down—by asking me if I "would look in on Vladimir's younger sister, who still lives in Prague." It turned out that Nabokov's widowed sister Olga, then sixty-seven, resided in the same district that I did: right behind the Prague Castle in Hradcany, a district that also housed (a block and a half from my home) the city headquarters for the Central Group of Soviet Troops Stationed on Czechoslovak Soil. Nabokov, who hadn't seen his sister for more than thirty years, was still sending her $50 a month. Olga's son (deceased) had married a Czech girl—and it was Olga's devotion to her Czech grandson that, above all, kept her in Prague despite the discomforts of being a Russian "of class origins" in what was now a Soviet colony held in check by the Red Army.

PRAGUE 1970

The grandma who came to dinner one cold Sunday had the same head, eyes, and chin as her brother—plus a fairly thick crown of brown hair. "It's all my own!" she began, without waiting to be complimented (as proud of her brown as her sister-in-law was of her white). She conversed with my family and me in Czech, French, and English—all with gargled *r's* and with the recurrent note of world-weary certainty that is the mark of émigrés including (to a slighter degree) her brother.

Though she had another married name, she ordered me to call her "Nabokovová" and to "tell me, before I even take off my coat, what my brother is like."

Her intense curiosity about the brother she hadn't seen for some three decades barely lasted until we sat down in our living room. For Olga Nabokovová wanted to chat about *beaux-arts*. She had arrived a little out of breath from the official "Days of Soviet Culture"—a month-long "festival" that most Czechs were boycotting. "How," she asked me, "could I resist the show of 'Russian Art from the Hermitage'—from my own native city?" Before I could answer, she was describing the exhibition and then discoursing on Yugoslav religious wood-carving.

The tide of talk-about-the-arts swept to the dinner table, where I worked the names of Nora Kaye and Margot Fonteyn in edgewise. Olga Nabokovová suddenly said: "But, as for men dancers, it always strikes me as laughable when men go up on their toes." Here, she made a little finger ballet and both my children began to giggle. "Well, she went on, "it isn't at all masculine, is it?"

"But you do have to admire Nureyev!" I managed to protest. By then however, our guest was laughing infectiously and so were my children and so was my wife and so I found myself laughing, too, at the very idea of a man dancing!

MONTREUX 1971

"But that's incredible!" Vladimir Nabokov exclaimed a few months later when I told him about that conversation. "because that's almost exactly what my mother used to say about 'male ballerinas.'" He stared into his gin-and-tonic, apparently unable to fathom why good things die while prejudices endure.*

We were back in the Green Room on a winter afternoon. Véra Nabokov said to me: "Olga wrote to us that you never invited her back and she was very angry with you. But I wrote to her that you'd been expelled from Czechoslovakia soon after she saw you." Then Véra riveted me with the stare that precedes a pronouncement: "You are a bright young man, but you have one failing in perception: the places you've picked to live. First Prague; now Vienna. The Austrians were worse than the Germans. We never travel in those countries."

---

*When my article containing these conversations about the dance appeared in the New York Times Magazine (October 31, 1971), it occasioned a learned letter-to-the-editor (published November 21) from a New Yorker with the fine Slavic name of Valentina Litvinoff pointing out that, while dancing *en pointe* is ballet's stock-in-trade it is strictly a female technique. Since men in ballet do not, as a rule, dance on toe, neither Nabokov's mother nor his sister "could have seen the spectacle they so pejoratively discuss." Ms. Litvinoff noted, however, that an entirely different form uses men on toe: Georgian folk dance: "Supported by their fitted boots, their knees flexed like goats—and just as nimble—these dancers have long been acclaimed for the masculine virility which imbues their art." Reverting to ballet, Ms. Litvinoff proclaimed a recent exception to the rule: in his film, *The Tales of Beatrix Potter*, Sir Frederick Ashton put a dancing male pig on toe. "As for the Nabokovs," Ms. Litvinoff concluded, "their remarks serve to demonstrate once again that often even cultured people are lopsided in their awareness—and prove to be ignoramuses when it comes to dance."

(Adolph Eichmann, handed a copy of *Lolita* to read in his cell in Jerusalem, remarked: "That is quite an offensive book.")

Véra Nabokov's words were punctuated by a jolting thump from above. In the off-season, workmen on scaffolding were painting and pummeling the turreted façade of the Montreux-Palace while others were drilling the hotel's sturdy base.

"Isn't that disgraceful!" she exclaimed. "The hotel shouldn't rent rooms when they're making this kind of noise."

"That last was not the noise of workmen, my dear," her husband interjected. "That was the noise of small American children."

"How do you know?" I asked the author of *Lolita*.

"They run differently, they play differently, and they fall differently from European children."

(For a period of a year, the Nabokov's overhead neighbors in the Montreux-Palace were Peter Ustinov and his children. Ustinov says he "hated hotel living, but the place is absolutely right for Nabokov. You could do all of *Ada* right there—and he probably did. Our families got on well together; he and I spoke Russian and I often played Ping-Pong with his son Dmitri. Ustinov, who now owns an estate and vineyard on the other side of Lausanne, has a chalet in territory where Nabokov sometimes goes butterfly-hunting. "I got to my chalet one day not long ago," Ustinov told me, "to find, scratched in pencil near the door, 'NABOKOV VISITED.' I've since put that scratching under glass—like a poor butterfly."

The subject of children returned again, fleetingly, when we talked about the Nabokovs' empire upstairs on the hotel's sixth floor. Véra Nabokov started to describe it thusly: "Seven rooms, including two libraries, plus three bathrooms and four telephones and we're starting to outgrow all that. The furniture is a joke—"

"Except for my marvelous wooden lectern," said Vladimir Nabokov, referring to his living-room rostrum at which he usually writes (on index cards) standing up from shortly after 5:30 A.M. until 3:30 P.M. (Whenever he feels "gravity nibbling at my calves," he sinks into a trusted old armchair.) "The hotel found the lectern somewhere and gave it to us soon after we moved in. It was used by Flaubert once."

"Is that what makes it marvelous?" I asked him.

Véra Nabokov answered: "It's Louis Quinze or something, but it's broken."

"It's very old and very shaky," her husband conceded, "but it's not broken."

"Well, there's a crack in the connecting wood between two legs," Véra argued.

"Let's just say," said he, "that the legs are the weakest part. Looking at it, I can only guess that some Early American child came over to Europe and set about systematically kicking it to pieces."

She said: "As soon as it finally goes, I have the name of an excellent carpenter who made something like it for Mr. James Mason. But we hesitate to order it now."

"No need, no need," said he—and I think I caught a glimmer of superstition behind his words.

> Q: What are the author of *Lolita*'s present-day feelings about little American children?
>
> A: I don't know any.

Vladimir Nabokov referred my further questions about how he works to a 1964 *Playboy* interview he granted to author Alvin Toffler *(Future Shock)*. In it, Nabokov, reading prepared answers from his index cards, told Toffler:

"I do not begin my novel at the beginning. I do not reach chapter three before I reach chapter four. I do not go dutifully from one page to the next, in consecutive order; no, I pick out a bit here and a bit there, till I have filled all the gaps on paper. That is why I like writing my stories and novels on index cards, numbering them later when my whole set is complete. Every card is rewritten many times. About three cards make one typewritten page, and when finally I feel that the conceived picture has been copied by me as faithfully as physically possible—a few vacant lots always remain alas—then I dictate the novel . . ."

My questions had shifted since our first meeting because in the interim I'd been commissioned to write an article about Nabokov from my peculiar perspective. Nabokov's initial response to the project was one of casual indifference, "You know," he said, "if I'd ever wished to be a journalist, it would have been to cover Manson. The trial fascinates me. So much has been made of it."

"Yes," I said. "Even the President of the United States gets into the act to pronounce him guilty."*

---

*Charles Manson and three of his female followers were later sentenced to die in a California gas chamber (though the death penalty has not been effected there in recent years) for the ritual murders of pregnant actress Sharon Tate (Mrs. Roman Polanski) and six other victims. On August 4, 1970, while Manson was on trial, President Richard M. Nixon uttered *his* judgment: "Here is a man who is guilty, directly or indirectly, of eight murders without reason."

"Well, he was absolutely right to do that!" Nabokov snapped back. "If I were President, I'd have done it, too. Manson and those girls—they're cretins! They're not capable of thought. *[mimicking mincingly]* 'We stuck the forks into her stomach so that her baby would never have to fight in the war.' *[answering back fiercely]* What war?"

"The war in Vietnam," I guessed.

"Do you think those girls and Manson ever knew anything about the war in Vietnam? Yes, it exists, it's an idea to them, but it's hardly perceived. They talk about it, but they have no idea what they're talking about."

Inevitably, Manson generated a three-way argument, in which naught was pinned down. I spoke from my conscience as a journalist, recognizing that "our thirst for colorful copy creates not only cretins—your word, sir— like Manson and Sirhan Sirhan [assassin of Senator Robert F. Kennedy], but the glory we grant them also inspires a certain cult of 'dumb intellectuals' who are quite ready to pass shallow verdicts of life-and-death on strangers."

"Do you honestly believe that?" said Mrs. Nabokov, impaling me again with her stare of judgment. "Only someone on drugs could be reached by a Manson. Why do you call them a cult? . . . I favor hanging them."

Her husband, the author of *Invitation to a Beheading*, said he opposed capital punishment, but added that "if the aim of jail is rehabilitation, you cannot rehabilitate such people. Certainly, they should be caged for life."

She said: "Then they'll be out in twelve years. They're too dangerous. I was listening to the radio the other day and there was some baboon of a film producer in Paris saying 'Manson expressed what a lot of us are feeling. We're all behind you, Charlie!' "

"There!" I said. "Doesn't that indicate Manson's influence extends beyond his 'Family'—and is spread by the media?"

"The baboon must have been on drugs, too," she answered.

"Even so," her husband pointed out, "we have friends who fit the description of 'dumb intellectuals.' " He whispered a name to his wife and then told her and me: "That couple is perfectly capable of coming out and saying something outrageous like 'We're all behind you, Charlie.'"

"*She* isn't, though *he* might," Mrs. Nabokov admitted inconclusively.

> Q: We talked . . . about the Manson case, but I never did find out why and *how* it

fascinates you or why it made you wish for once to be a journalist.

A: I have a taste for case histories and it would have interested me greatly to look for one spark of remorse in that moronic monster and his moronic beast girls. I would have been also interested to find more about the cretins who "admire" those brutes.

Q: As one American to another, where do you stand on Vietnam?

A: All I know is that I would not like S. Vietnam to turn into Sovietnam, and that blunders do not win wars.

When I brought the subject back to my own journalistic mission of profiling Nabokov, a slightly on-the-record intonation entered the conversation.

"I'll be happy to cooperate, but there *is* one difficulty," Nabokov said. "I insist on the questions being asked in writing, so I can answer in writing. Because I don't talk too well—"

I interrupted with a fervent protest and an assurance that he was such a good speaker that I wished *I'd* had him for my college lecturer.

"Well," said Nabokov, "then maybe I talk too much and sometimes I say very foolish things. So I need to have my index cards before me with written answers prepared . . . Oh, I can elaborate on them, of course, but I have to be careful.

"No so long ago," he went on, "I had an interviewer with a tape recorder and it went well for several days—an hour a day— all done from *his* questions and *my* index cards. Then, on his last night in Montreux, he took us to dinner at a country inn. He fed me a good many drinks and, after a while, I stopped looking at my index cards and then, when I did look for them, I couldn't find them. But I was feeling good, so I went on talking—and, apparently, his tape kept going and going. I had a perfectly fine time—until my wife told me the next day what I'd said."

"By then, the man was gone," Véra Nabokov added ominously, "and it took a good deal of cabling and phoning before we could find him and get some of it deleted."

"But," said her husband blissfully, "they kept the sound of the church bell tolling in the village. I was glad of that!"

The bell I heard tolling was a warning buzzer. Before further restrictions could be imposed, I quickly agreed to submit my formal questions in writing, but nothing was said about our informal conversations or my research or field work. And, in the interests of informality, I suggested that, when I rejoined the Nabokovs next, it ought to be for butterfly-hunting. Nabokov took to the idea. Though it was still Alpine winter, butterflies danced in the margin of our dialogue from then on.

Just the day before, he had played hooky from his writing lectern to shop for shorts in Lausanne, fourteen miles away, in anticipation of the next butterfly season. He had been looking for "something younger and narrower than heretofore," though not the "hot pants" the tailor had dared to dangle before him:

"The tailor and I talked for more than an hour, although we didn't settle everything. So I suppose I must make another trip to Lausanne before spring comes. Why, I talk about a trip to Lausanne the way others talk about a trip to Hawaii! Well, I only get over to Lausanne once or twice a year, though I go to New York or London or Rome oftener.

"When I left the tailor, I went right to the station and took the first train back to Montreux. It was a local and it was probably the first Swiss train in history that was ever late. Took more than an hour. It was an awful trip!"

"That," said Vera Nabokov, "is the difference between you and me. I would wait for the next express train, while you'll take the local just because it's there."

"For all its troubles, though," her husband purred, "my local train arrived in Montreux before the first express."

> Q: [Professor] Morris Bishop [who brought Nabokov from Wellesley to Cornell] recalls: "I was fascinated not only by the range and depth of Vladimir's knowledge but by his exclusions. He had small interest in politics, none in society's economic concerns. He cared nothing for problems of low-cost housing, school consolidation, bond issues for sewage-treatment plants. He got the news not from the New York *Times*, but from the *Daily News*, quivering with wickedness, lust, and bloodshed. He subscribed for a time to Father Divine's periodical,

revelatory of a lurid, exalted world. His study was rather of human behavior and misbehavior than the pratings of men in power."

Nowadays, in Switzerland, what are your sources of information about the outside world?

A: My old friend Morris Bishop is a great stylist and he has brought up the "Father Divine's periodical" on a wave of style. I don't think I ever read it.

Nowadays, in Switzerland, I dip into quite a number of periodicals: *The Herald Tribune, The National Review, The New York Review of Books, Time, Newsweek, The Saturday Review, The New Yorker, Playboy, Esquire, Encounter, The Listener, The Spectator, The New Statesman, Punch,* the London Sunday papers and so forth.

VIENNA — MONTREUX

All spring, my questions and Nabokov's answers spilled through the mails, while covering letters scheduled and rescheduled our butterfly hunt. A rendezvous in Sicily in late April or early May was canceled because of Italy's spring strike epidemic. An early summer meeting in Lenzerheide (in the German-speaking part of Switzerland) was confirmed and reconfirmed; hotels were booked; and then all was undone when Vera Nabokov took sick. A bad reaction to antibiotics for various ailments had put her into a Geneva hospital and, now that she was out, a fortnight of bed rest had left her with circulatory trouble in her feet. Nabokov stayed home with her and their summer evenings were spent on their Montreux terrace (overlooking lake Geneva) with him reading to her, in Russian, Alexander Solzhenitsyn's *August, 1914.* And (here comes a bit of journalistic straddling) who will deny that, from the Arbors of Ardis, there issued wild cackles of laughter at the manly prose of this tragic, heroic political figure who, at the time, was refusing to run the risk of going to Sweden to accept his Nobel Prize for fear that Soviet Russia might force him into emigration?

Q: "My private tragedy, which cannot and indeed should not, be anybody's concern, is that I had to abandon my natural idiom, my untrammeled, rich, and infinitely docile Russian tongue for a second-rate brand of English . . ."

Can you pinpoint or generalize *when* you think in English and *when* you think in Russian?

A: Unless one actually recollects or devises sentences, spoken or written, one thinks in images, not in languages (and this is why Bloom's mental soliloquy is a stylized exaggeration, a delightful kind of delirium). If I am asked "do you remember that conversation we had the other day?", it comes back to me in a shapeless flash. The blur may be flavored with French, or tinged with Russian, or soaked in American—that depends solely on the tongue in which the conversation had been conducted—and a phrase I wish to recall or cannot help recalling may stand out with full verbal precision; but that is all. The same occurs if I say to myself "I know what I shall tell Ivan Ivanovich" (who happens to be a profound monolinguist) or "I know what old François (another unfortunate) will reply." To put it in a coconut shell, the actual words (both mine and his) are framed by the lips of the mind if there is intent or retroanalysis but the choice of language itself has no psychological significance; and of course an imagined tower or tree stands speechless.

MONTREUX 1971

With Nabokov's chauffeur disabled and his auto garaged for repairs, I have hired a public taxicab for our butterfly expedition to the bird sanctuary at Grangette, six miles from Montreux. And,

Bozhe moy! (Russian for "good Heavens!"), an unwittingly jocose dispatcher has sent us a Russian émigré cabbie: Mme. Natalie Green-Skariatine, a Tartar who has "been out since 1920 and driving for thirty-nine years." The lady has driven the Nabokovs twice or thrice before, also by coincidence. The very first time, her passengers were discussing a confidential family matter in Russian—thinking this would afford them privacy. Sensing the situation, the driver had interrupted them with a Russian greeting: "And where is God carrying you?"

Thus, today's conversation en route is in Russian and it carries us, without a glance by Nabokov, past the lakeside castle at Chillon (of whose prisoners Byron sang) and past the perch-eating tourists of Villeneuve. When we dismount, however, Nabokov tells Mme. Green-Skariatine where to wait. Now all eyes are for butterflies. "Over here!" says Nabokov. "The underbrush is most tempting."

His quest today is for "a very interesting butterfly" called 'Purple Emperor.' After calling for "silence, not total silence, but some silence," he describes "its beautiful violet sheen—if you turn it this way and that way, the shimmer changes. It used to fly here until they asphalted this road. Now it's getting scarcer and scarcer. I saw one the other day up in Caux—but I couldn't look at it closer because it was flying higher and higher in such a hurry—*Ahhhhh!*"

With a whooshing left backhand swoop, Nabakov bags a lemonish yellow butterfly and holds his throbbing net up for inspection.

"A brimstone, not uncommon," he explains. "This was supposed to be the first butterfly ever noticed: hence the name *butter*fly. Another version has it that the name was derived from *flutter by*—making it all a Spoonerism!"

The author of *The Gift* opens his net and lets his captive go. Rather relieved, I congratulate the old tennis teacher on his backhand.

"I'm glad you appreciated that," he says. "It's not easy to take a flying butterfly—because it dodges. The best way is to wait for it to settle on a flower—or on damp earth, it's quite easy to take." He confesses to "a little spring training in the room," though more out of anticipation than necessity.

Nabokov's next catch—made in a more orthodox creep-and-pounce, if not cat-and-mouse, manner— is a gray Veined White, which he extracts from his net, holds up gingerly, and croons over: "So pale! ... A very common butterfly that gradually grades into an Alpine form."

"Please explain," I ask, as Nabokov sets it free, too.

"If you go up certain hills and mountains for about eighteen hundred meters you'll find a peculiarly beautiful gray-yellowish version of this—but, all along the way up, you'll encounter intermediate forms. This one and that one fly differently and have different caterpillars, but you can see the changes as you go."

"Like walking through a very detailed catalog," I remark appreciatively.

"Good simile!" says Nabokov, definitely *on*stage, as though dishing out a tennis compliment. "You can put it in quotes and give it to me."

For the next quarter-hour, the pickings are slim and the hunt bogs down in swampy underbrush. Nabokov concedes: "We'll go back to our starting point and take a different turn. I would say that, after a promising start, I lost the first set, six to three."

Early in the second set, Nabokov slaps at his left leg and says: "That was a deer fly—Western U.S. for what *you* call a horse fly. It takes a very big and painful bite, but usually there are no bad effects... Here, there are also vipers—but a little later in the season. Their bites are not fatal—unless you're ill or old or very young." And, since he is none of these, Nabokov says no more about vipers, but moves on to bigger challenges:

"I have walked among rattlesnakes. Yes, in Arizona, when I was writing the screenplay for *Lolita*. We would take my index cards in the morning and go out collecting and writing until lunch. And, one day, I remember killing an immense rattler that was just lying in wait for us when we came out toward the road. I was the first to hear its hysterical rattlings. Vera almost stepped on it, but I held her back. Then I picked up a piece of lead piping and smashed the thing. A moment later, I saw its female slithering away. Vera called me 'St. George' for quite a while after that!"

From the perils of making a movie out of *Lolita* a decade earlier, the talk gravitates to Alan Jay Lerner's and John Barry's musical stage version, *Lolita, My Love*, which aborted on its way to Broadway that spring. Sight unseen ("but I have spies I incited to go see it"), Nabokov announces that "both girls—the one they fired and the one who replaced her—were awful: little bosomy girls, the wrong type altogether."

"Don't you retain any artistic control over such things?" I ask.

"None whatsoever. I reason this way: if they're going to do it some day, they're going to do it. So I had better be around when

they do it—not only to criticize the thing, but also to explain that I have nothing to do with it."

He flails at a moving butterfly and misses—but he has few regrets: "Not a rare butterfly, that one, but a spectacular one. The kind that a boy collector is very anxious to take."

Dodging an occasional motorbike, we press on down a black-topped road. Suddenly, with an "Oh-oh!," Nabokov swishes his net behind him and clasps it with both hands. I look to see what he has bagged now—but he shushes me away and, all guile, *bonjours* a disinterested official wearing a box-hatted gray uniform.

As soon as the official has passed, Nabokov switches the net from back to chest and explains: "That was a ranger. I musn't show my net in a nature preserve. Not that they could prove I'm catching butterflies. Or even identify a butterfly I was chasing . . ."

Then, for the next three minutes, I am serenaded with an imagined courtroom scene in which the wily author of *The Defense* runs rings about befuddled bureaucrats who have him on trial for attempting to exterminate the cabbage butterfly. The trial continues, with one digression for rerouting ("Let's turn off here. The dimmer the place, the better the butterfly"), and then a sudden-death ending—*Lash!*

"This one I will take," says Nabokov. "A lovely intergrade between the common Veined White and its cousin Bryony White. Could you ever hear me explaining *that* subtlety to the ranger?"

Out of Nabokov's jacket pocket comes a Band-Aid box. Into a little glassine envelope, similar to those favored by stamp collectors, goes the butterfly. Into the Band-Aid box goes the envelope and back into Nabokov's pocket goes the Band-Aid box.

"The butterfly in the Band-Aid box—?" I begin.

"An *old* Band-Aid box," he says, laughing. "That envelope will hold the butterfly until I want to spread it. In there I can keep my butterflies for years and years, hundreds of years. When I am ready, I have only to relax them between wet towels and leave them overnight—and the next day pin them—"

"But the one in there now?" I persist. "Is it still alive?"

"Oh, you didn't see me pinching it under the net? That killed it, though sometimes I have to repinch them. When Véra's with me, she keeps an eagle eye on them. She hates to see half-dead butterflies."

With a "lovely intergrade" to take home to his ailing wife, Nabokov is soon willing to give up on his initial objective, the Purple Emperor. He admits that he was seeking it for sentimental reasons:

"I just remember many places with it. As a boy, I hunted it in Bad Kissingen in Bavaria, but now I think that splendid butterfly is extinct. No, not entirely extinct; some are still seen in the New Forest in England and . . . in Northern France. If it were a much smaller butterfly, people would think it extinct. There are so few left, but it's a question of size. If you don't see something, it's extinct, but if you see just one of it, then it isn't."

Pondering the paradoxes of extinction and immortality—and perhaps marveling at how he has steered his own steady course between them in more than half a century of exile—Vladimir Nabokov returns to our waiting taxi. Mme. Green-Skariatine has it pointed toward Montreux with the motor running.

"Was it a successful day?" she asks us in English.

Beckoning knowingly toward me, Nabokov confides: "From *his* point of view, it was successful. From *mine*, well, I've had better days."

Later in the week, Nabokov will excuse himself to "go into hiding" and finish his next novel, *Transparent Things* (1972). "Does this week," I ask him in the cab, "mean the last butterflies of summer?"

"Oh, I think not, I hope not!" says Vladimir Nabokov, rubbing his hands with the glee of anticipation. *"Transparent Things* is very nearly done and then I have a rendezvous with The Butterfly on the Simplon on the fifteenth of next month."

EPILOGUE

I might have known how our friendship could end. John Updike had observed that Nabokov's "implacable hatreds" and "reflexive contempt" were "the least warming aspects of his image." Herbert Gold, who was Nabokov's "temporary successor" at Cornell, later interviewed him for *Paris Review* and *The Saturday Evening Post*. Gold was treated cordially in Montreux, but Nabokov subsequently wrote a letter to the editor of *Satevepost* denouncing Gold. But I had no idea how serious or accurate or justified or petty these backbites could be, though I strove to avoid the sterile form of written questions-and-answers Nabokov favored because I agreed with nature writer and novelist Edward Hoagland's lament (in *The Village Voice*) that "Nabokov is too wordy and foppish in interviews."

My article, "Understanding Vladimir Nabokov: A Red Autumn Leaf Is a Red Autumn Leaf, Not a Deflowered Nymphet," condensed slightly from this basic account, was spread across eleven pages of the New York *Times Magazine* for Halloween, 1971, in among ads for Country Cuddler Coats and Natural Russian Sable designed on Seventh Avenue; Cheri-Suisse Swiss Chocolate Cherry Liqueur and "Ma Griffe, the perfume that allows a woman to test herself"; Hygrolett Air Humidifiers and Farberware ("Choose a pot like you choose a husband"). Copies mailed to the Nabokovs at the Montreux-Palace did not evoke any comment or complaint. In early 1972, a prepublication copy of my book *Rowboat to Prague* was sent to the Nabokovs, too, with all good wishes and the usual vain hope of eliciting a quotable blurb. Instead it provoked a letter from *Mrs. N.* conveying her husband's thanks for sending the book, "certainly a valuable historic testimony." Véra Nabokov went on to say that she would have written sooner if her husband had not been "somewhat upset" by my article; in fact, she added, "I ought to be even more frank and say that he was not just 'somewhat upset' but 'very upset.' " She said, however, that it would be pointless at such a late date to enumerate the "various distressing items," but that her husband did want her to put his upset on record. She ended by wishing my family and me happiness in Vienna, but one of us was a little less happy and wondered what he had done wrong.

Two months later I found my profile denounced by Nabokov in the pages of the April 15, 1972, *Vogue,* of all places—in a special travel issue featuring "SOPHIA LOREN tells her travel secrets" and "VLADIMIR NABOKOV talks about his travels." To the first question ("What is there in Montreux that attracts you?") the "world's most inspired and observant traveler as well as its greatest living writer" briefly mentioned the people, the mountains, the mails, and the hotel, where "our quarters consist of several tiny rooms with *two and a half bathrooms, the result of two apartments having been recently fused. The sequence is: kitchen, living-dining room, my wife's room, my room, a former kitchenette now full of my papers, and our son's room. The apartment is cluttered with books, folders, and files. What might be termed rather grandly a library is a back room housing my published work, and there are additional shelves in the attic* whose skylight is much frequented by pigeons and alpine choughs. I am giving this meticulous description to refute a distortion in an interview published recently in another New York magazine—a long piece with embarrassing misquotations, wrong intonations, and false exchanges in the course of which I am made to dismiss the scholarship of a dear friend as 'pedantry' and to poke ambiguous fun at a manly writer's tragic fate."

The italics above are mine—to show the extent of *my* distortion when I quoted Mrs. Nabokov earlier in these pages and in The New York *Times*' as saying their quarters consisted of "seven rooms, including *two libraries, plus three bathrooms* and four telephones . . ." Her husband's own description justifies two libraries. The differences between two-and-a-half and three bathrooms would be hard enough to calculate with the naked eye. But I had to leave it for Mr. and Mrs. N. to negotiate, for while I was once told I would have a chance to see their place, I was not invited up there even when I asked to be. *Tant pis!*, as Humbert Humbert might not ejaculate.

I suspect the living quarters were merely a point of departure in the columns of *Vogue*, and I am sure Nabokov took his other two specific objections much more seriously. But I must stand by both the quotation about Alfred Appel and the nonquotation about Solzhenitsyn. For the first, I had a witness. With regard to Solzhenitsyn, I still have the exact quote about how he reads in Russian (and, again, I have a witness), but I knew Nabokov was sorry the moment he said it. Sure enough, a minute or two later, Nabokov informed me it had been off the record. I felt no obligation—because the ethic I was taught at Columbia Journalism (and which I have practiced) is that if something is to be put off the record, it must be done so beforehand (giving me the chance to say either "O.K." or, as I've sometimes said, "No, don't tell me and I'll find it out my own way"). In this instance, I said I would "try to oblige" and later arrived at this compromise with myself: Nabokov's literary opinion of any Russian writer was a particularly valuable one that I couldn't leave out altogether. So I made it into a stylized hint of either his or his wife's taste in best-sellers.

As it turned out, I wasn't blazing any incontrovertibly new trail. In a Q&A interview made a few weeks before my butterfly hunt with Nabokov, but published more than two months after my profile appeared, Israel Shenker (in "The Old Magician At Home," New York *Times Book Review*, January 9, 1972, p.2) handled the same problem in much the same way: lapsing out of quotes and into paraphrase. "No," wrote Shenker, "he cannot take seriously the rage for Solzhenitsyn's writing. An inferior author, he says; but he is waiting for the latest Solzhenitsyn book in Russian."

Making feuds is not what Shenker or I were about. It is certainly not what two unique makers of literature, Nabokov and

Solzhenitsyn, whose pasts complement each other and who both landed in Switzerland, should ever be about.* In the style of Romain Rolland's *Colas Breugnon*, which Nabokov translated into Russian in 1922 as *Nikola Persik*, good men still live—inside and outside Soviet Russia. And, in the words of an old poet Nabokov invented and Humbert quoted:
> "The moral sense in mortals is the duty
> We have to pay on mortal sense of beauty."

Into his seventy-seventh year, Vladimir Nabokov continued to walk and run ten or fifteen miles on a spring or summer day in quest of the elusive butterfly, but a mysterious malady had been slowly taking its toll and, gradually, running slowed to walking and net gave way to cane. Pronounced clinically cured by doctors in the U.S. and Switzerland several times, he would nonetheless emerge visibly weaker from each bout of hospitalization and soon the fever would strike again. For a while, he and Vera moved up the high hill above Montreux to live at Valmont, the fashionable *clinique médicale, diététique et physiothérapique* that, until Claudia Cardinale shed eleven pounds there in eight days making ready for a movie role, had been best known as the place Rainer Maria Rilke died in 1926 after pricking his finger on a rose. (Rilke already had leukemia.)

Back at the Montreux-Palace, he still went for walks, "not the alpine rambles of previous years," his son Dimitri recalls, "but a few hundred feet, up and down the Grand Rue. Father always had a cheerful quip for the druggist and news-vendor, and never once complained of his weakness. The last time we had had a good tramp together in the mountains had been at Rougemont, near Gstaad, a couple of summers before. He told me then, in one of those rare moments when father and son discuss such matters, that he had accomplished what he wished in life and art and was a truly happy man. His writing, he went on, was all there, ready inside his mind, like film waiting to be developed" and gradually coming to life: a sensation, the senior Nabokov noted, akin to Schopenhauer's vision of events as they unfold.

As a singer, Dmitri Nabokov is especially sensitive to breezes, drafts, and gusts — and he blames a chill wind that greeted him upon leaving the Grand Théâtre in Geneva one midnight of a

---
*When Solzhenitsyn finally was deported from his native Russia in 1973, Nabokov made quick contact and invited him to Montreux. Solzhenitsyn settled in Zürich for a year before moving to the U.S.

balmy March in 1977 for a virus that bedded first him and then his mother. "Although I had begged my parents not to come close," Dmitri recalls, "that evening my gentle father padded into my room with a trayful of food and a volume of de Musset for me to read. A couple of days later his voice grew husky, and he started clearing his throat more often than usual; but for several days he insisted he was fine.

"Soon, however, he was bedridden with a climbing temperature. Then it was the ambulance again, the Lausanne hospital with its doctors (who again announced that they had finally isolated the germ), the prospect of discharge in a few days, and the relapses, and Father's kind, still hopeful eyes, when he told me he was proud of me as I left for my Munich opera début."

Vladimir Nabokov was once more at at home in his hotel when Dmitri rejoined his parents in Montreux that June, but the fever returned and soon the senior Nabokov was back in Lausanne Hospital. This time, Dmitri noted, "the air of condescending reassurance had disappeared, and one had the troubling sensation that the physicians' manner was changing from bedside to graveside." Upon a brief return home, "the end was quick: a chance draft from door and window simultaneously left open by an incautious, sneezing maid. Bronchial congestion suddenly more severe. The powerful heart that had endured strain after strain stilled with an abrupt threefold moan; the mind that loved life to the last, extinguished."

The date was Saturday, July 2, 1977, ten weeks after Nabokov's seventy-eighth birthday, but his son prefers to remember a penultimate farewell a few days earlier, "after I had kissed his still-warm forehead—as I had for years when saying goodnight or goodbye—tears suddenly welled in Father's eyes. I asked him why. He replied that a certain butterfly was already on the wing; and his eyes told me he no longer hoped that he would live to pursue it again."

2
"INVENT THE WORLD! INVENT REALITY!":
A PORTRAIT in QUOTES

(When a quotation in italics is not otherwise attributed, it is by Vladimir Nabokov.)

BORN APRIL 1899: *"All dates are given in the New Style: we lagged twelve days behind the rest of the civilized world in the nineteenth century, and thirteen in the beginning of the twentieth. By the Old Style I was born on 10 April, at daybreak, in the last year of the last century, and that was (if I could have been whisked across the border at once) 22 April in, say, Germany; but since all my birthdays were celebrated, with diminishing pomp, in the twentieth century, everybody, including myself, upon being shifted by revolution and expatriation from the Julian calendar to the Gregorian, used to add thirteen, instead of twelve days to the 10th of April. The error is serious. What is to be done? I find '23 April' under 'birth date' in my most recent passport, which is also the birth date of Shakespeare, my nephew Vladimir Sikorski, Shirley Temple and Hazel Brown (who, moreover, shares my passport). This, then, is the problem. Calculatory ineptitude prevents me from trying to solve it."*

—From 1966 foreword to autobiography, *Speak, Memory*

★ ★ ★ ★ ★ ★ ★ ★

"I will relate you exactly what occurred on this occasion and I think that you might find joy in my recounting of it. I will narrate the following: I saw him doing the most extraordinary things, which I could hardly give him credit for. I said, 'What are you about?' 'Nothing,' he replied, astonished by my observation. He raised one eyebrow into that indeterminate space between his hairline and the green globe of his eye. 'Why,' he mused, 'do you ask?' "

—Peter Ustinov's parody of Nabokov's style (Mallorca, July, 1972), accompanied by the following observation by Ustinov: "He writes English in such a perfumed and extraordinarily able way and speaks it extremely well, but one can detect the traces of early Victorian Scottish nanny."

"In that summer of 1918, a poor little oasis of miraged youth, . . . A bantering friendship soon developed between my coeval Lidia T. and me . . . Lidia and I played a little oasal game of our own invention. The idea consisted of parodizing a biographic approach projected, as it were, into the future and thus transforming the very specious pre-

sent into a kind of paralyzed past as perceived by a doddering memoirist who recalls, through a helpless haze, his acquaintance with a great writer when both were young. For instance, either Lidia or I (it was a matter of chance inspiration), might say, on the terrace after supper: 'The writer liked to go out on the terrace after supper' or 'I shall always remember the remark V. V. made one warm night: 'It is,' he remarked, "a warm night"; or, still sillier:'He was in the habit of lighting his cigarette, before smoking it' —all this delivered with much pensive, reminiscent fervor which seemed hilarious and harmless to us at the time; but now—now I catch myself wondering if we did not disturb unwittingly some perverse and spiteful demon."
—From chapter 12 of *Speak, Memory*

"An extraordinary grand-aunt, Baroness Bredow, born Tolstoy, amply replaced closer blood. As a child of seven or eight, already harboring the secrets of a confined madman, I seemed even to her (who also was far from normal) unduly sulky and indolent; actually, of course, I kept daydreaming in a most outrageous fashion.

" 'Stop moping!' she would cry: 'Look at the harlequins!'

" 'What harlequins? Where?'

" 'Oh, everywhere. All around you. Trees are harlequins, words are harlequins. So are situations and sums. Put two things together— jokes, images—and you get a triple harlequin. Come on! Play! Invent the world! Invent reality!'

"I did. By Jove, I did. I invented my grand-aunt in honor of my first daydreams, and now, down the marble steps of memory's front porch, here she slowly comes, sideways, sideways . . ."—From 1974 novel, *Look at the Harlequins!*

In his January 1964, *Playboy* interview with Nabokov, Alvin Toffler asked him if he believed in God. Nabokov replied:

"To be quite candid—and what I am going to say now is something I never said before, and I hope it provokes a salutary little chill: I know more than I can express in words, and the little I can express would not have been expressed, had I not known more."

* * * * * * * *

"I liked, as I like still, to make words look self-conscious and foolish, to bind them by the mock marriage of a pun, to turn them inside out, to come upon them unawares. What is this jest in majesty? This ass in passion? How do God and Devil combine to form a live dog?"
—From novel *Despair (Otchayanie)*, written in Russian in 1932 and later translated and revised by the author

> "Can one picture a blackbird
> as the negative of a small firebird?
> Can a record run backward,
> turn 'repaid' into 'diaper'?"
> —From 1955 poem, "Ode to a Model"

At the age of six, Vladimir Nabokov, while building a tower out of alphabet blocks, remarked that the colors were all wrong. Hearing this, his mother compared observations and discovered that some of her letters had the same tints; in addition, music notes affected her eyes. In chapter 2 of *Speak, Memory,* Nabokov also writes:

"*On top of all this I present a fine case of colored hearing ... The long* a *of the English alphabet ... has for me the tint of weathered wood, but a French* a *evokes polished ebony. This black group also includes hard* g *(vulcanized rubber) and* r *(a sooty rag being ripped). Oatmeal* n, *noodle-limp* l, *and the ivory-backed hand mirror of* o *take care of the whites ... Passing on to the blue group, there is steely* x, *thundercloud* z, *and huckleberry* k. *Since a subtle interaction exists between sound and shape, I see* q *as browner than* k, *while* s *is not the light blue of* c, *but a curious mixture of azure and mother-of-pearl ...*

"I hasten to complete my list before I am interrupted. In the green group, there are alder-leaf f, *the unripe apple of* p, *and pistachio* t. *Dull green, combined somehow with violet, is the best I can do for* w. *The yellows comprise various* e*'s and* i*'s, creamy* d, *bright-golden* y, *and* u *whose alphabetical value I can express only by 'brassy with an olive sheen.' In the brown group, there are the rich rubbery tone of soft* g, *paler* j, *and the drab shoelace of* h. *Finally, among the reds,* b *has the tone called burnt sienna by painters,* m *is a fold of pink flannel, and today I have at last perfectly matched* v *with 'Rose Quartz' in Maerz and Pauls's* Dictionary of Color. *The word for rainbow, a primary, but decidedly muddy, rainbow, is in my private language, the hardly pronounceable:* kzspygv. *The first author to discuss* audition coloree *was, as far as I know, an albino physician in 1812, in Erlangen."*

In noting that *Lolita*'s villain, Clare Quilty, is identified as a "red beast" or "red fiend" and that red is Quilty's color, annotator Alfred Appel, Jr., reminds his readers that Nabokov is no "symbolist." After reading a draft of Appel's notes, which had other red images, too, Nabokov contributed this "Note about Symbols and Colors re *Annotated Lolita,*" which Appel calls "one of the most signif'cant statements Nabokov has made about his own art":

"There exist novelists and poets, and ecclesiastic writers, who deliberately use color terms, or numbers, in a strictly symbolic sense. The type of writer I am, half-painter, half-naturalist, finds the use of symbols hateful because it substitutes a dead general idea for a live specific impression. I am therefore puzzled and distressed by the significance you lend to the general idea of 'red' in my book. When the intellect limits itself to the general notion, or primitive notion, of a certain color it deprives the sense of its shades. In different languages, different colors were used in a general sense before shades were distinguished. (In French, for example, the 'redness' of hair is now expressed by 'roux' *meaning rufous, or russet, or fulvous with a reddish cast.) For me, the shades, or rather colors of, say, a fox, a ruby, a carrot, a pink rose, a dark cherry, a flushed cheek, are as different as blue is from green or the royal purple of blood (Fr. 'pourpre') from the English sense of violet blue. I think your students, your readers, should be taught to see things, to discriminate between visual shades as the author does, and not to lump them under such arbitrary labels as 'red' (using it, moreover, as a sexual symbol, though actually the dominant shades in males are mauve—to bright blue, in certain monkeys) . . . Roses may be white, and even black-red. Only cartoonists, having three colors at their disposal, use red for hair, cheek and blood.*"

* * * * * * * *

". . . When a certain moth resembles a certain wasp in shape and color, it also walks and moves its antennae in a waspish, unmothlike manner. When a butterfly has to look like a leaf, not only are all the details of a leaf beautifully rendered but markings mimicking grub-bored holes are generously thrown in. 'Natural selection,' in the Darwinian sense, could not explain the miraculous coincidence of imitative aspect and imitative behavior, nor could one appeal to the theory of 'the struggle for life' when a protective device was carried to a point of mimetic subtlety, exuberance, and luxury far in excess of a predator's power of appreciation. I discovered in nature the nonutilitarian delights that I sought in art. Both were a form of magic, both were a game of intricate enchantment."—From *Speak, Memory*'s chapter 6, the most accessibly complete and perhaps poetic source of Nabokov on butterflies:

> "Wide open on its pin (though fast asleep),
> and safe from creeping relatives and rust,
> in the secluded stronghold where we keep
> type specimens it will transcend its dust."
> — From a 1943 ode to "A Discovery"

In 1944, reporting on one of his discoveries, *Lycaeides melissa samuelis Nabokov*, in taxonomical terms, lepidopterist Nabokov livened up his scholarly prose with a stylist's flutter: *"From the opposite side of the distally twinned uncus and facing each other in the manner of the stolidly raised fists of two pugilists (of the old school) with the uncus hoods lending a Ku Klux Klan touch to the picture . . ."*

"Once, as a grown man, I was under ether during appendectomy, and with the vividness of a decalcomania picture I saw my own self in a sailor suit mounting a freshly emerged Emperor moth under the guidance of a Chinese lady who I knew was my mother. It was all there, brilliantly reproduced in my dream, while my own vitals were being exposed: the soaking, ice-cold absorbent cotton pressed to the insect's lemurian head; the subsiding spasms of its body; the satisfying crackle produced by the pin penetrating the hard crust of its thorax; the careful insertion of the point of the pin in the cork-bottomed groove of the spreading board; the symmetrical adjustment of the thick, strong-veined wings under neatly affixed strips of semitransparent paper."

—From chapter 6 of *Speak, Memory*

TO THE STARTING POINT OF A BUTTERFLY HUNT: *"My favorite method of locomotion . . . is the cableway and especially the chair lift. I find it enchanting and dreamy in the best sense of the word to glide in the morning sun from valley to timberline in that magic seat and to watch from above my own shadow—with the ghost of a butterfly net in the ghost of a fist—as it keeps gently ascending in sitting profile along the flowerly slope below, among dancing Ringlets and skimming Fritillaries. Some day the butterfly hunter will find even finer dreamlore when floating upright over mountains, carried by a diminutive rocket strapped to his back."*

—Q&A interview with Simona Morini in *Vogue*,
(April 15, 1972)

". . . a 'lepist' indulging in his quiet quest was apt to provoke strange reactions in other creatures. How often, when a picnic had been arranged . . . some cousin or aunt of mine would remark: 'Must you really take that net with you? Can't you enjoy yourself like a normal boy? Don't you think you are spoiling everybody's pleasure?' Near a sign NACH BODENLAUBE, at Bad Kissingen, Bavaria, just as I was about to join for a long walk my father and majestic old Muromtsev (who, four years before, in 1906, had been President of the first Rus-

sian Parliament), the latter turned his marble head toward me, a vulnerable boy of eleven, and said with his famous solemnity: 'Come with us by all means, but do not chase butterflies, child. It spoils the rhythm of the walk.' On a path above the Black Sea in the Crimea, among shrubs in waxy bloom, in March 1918, a bow-legged Bolshevik sentry attempted to arrest me for signaling (with my net, he said) to a British warship. In the summer of 1929, every time I walked through a village in the Eastern Pyrenees, and happened to look back, I would see in my wake the villagers frozen in the various attitudes my passage had caught them in, as if I were Sodom and they Lot's wife. A decade later, in the Maritime Alps, I once noticed the grass undulate in a serpentine way behind me because a fat rural policeman was wriggling after me on his belly to find out if I were not trapping songbirds. America has shown even more of this morbid interest in my retiary activities than other countries have—perhaps because I was in my forties when I came there to live, and the older the man, the queerer he looks with a butterfly net in his hand. Stern farmers have drawn my attention to NO FISHING signs; from cars passing me on the highway have come wild howls of derision; sleepy dogs, though unmindful of the worst bum, have perked up and come at me, snarling; tiny tots have pointed me out to their puzzled mamas; broad-minded vacationists have asked me whether I was catching bugs for bait; and one morning on a wasteland, lit by tall yuccas in bloom, near Santa Fe, a big black mare followed me for more than a mile.

—From Chapter 6 of *Speak, Memory*

* * * * * * * *

When *Playboy* interviewer Toffler asked Nabokov what he read in his youth, he was told:

"Between the ages of 10 and 15 in St. Petersburg, I must have read more fiction and poetry—English, Russian, and French—than in any other five year period of my life. I relished especially the works of Wells, Poe, Browning, Keats, Flaubert, Verlaine, Rimbaud, Chekhov, Tolstoy, and Alexander Blok. On another level, my heroes were the Scarlet Pimpernel, Phileas Fogg, and Sherlock Holmes. In other words, I was a perfectly normal trilingual child in a family with a large library. At a later period, in Cambridge, England, between the ages of 20 and 23, my favorites were Housman, Rupert Brooke, Joyce, Proust and Pushkin ... I was never exposed in the 20s and 30s, as so many of my coevals have been, to the poetry of Eliot and Pound. I read them late in the season, around 1945, in the guest room of an American friend's house, and not only remained completely indifferent to them, but could not understand why anybody should bother about them. But I suppose that they preserve some sentimental value for such readers as discovered them at an earlier age than I did."

"When I was thirteen we were playing hide-and-seek once and I and another boy of the same age found ourselves hiding together in a wardrobe. In the darkness he told me that there were marvelous beauties who allowed themselves to be undressed for money. I didn't properly hear what he called them and I thought it was 'prinstitute'—a mixture of princess and young ladies' institute. So I had an entrancing, mysterious mental image of them. But then of course I soon realized how mistaken I had been because I saw nothing attractive about the women who strolled up and down the Nevski rolling their hips and called us high-school boys 'pencils.'

—Ganin to Podtyagin in chapter 5 of
Nabokov's first novel, *Mary* (1926)

★ ★ ★ ★ ★ ★ ★ ★

"To the left, in the murky, mysterious distance, shimmered the diamond lights of Yalta. And when Martin would turn, he saw the flaming, restless nest of the fire a short distance away, and the silhouettes of people around it, and someone's hand adding a branch. The crickets kept crepitating; from time to time there came a secret whiff of burning juniper; and, above the black alpestrine steppe, above the silken sea, the enormous, all-engulfing sky, dove-gray with stars, made one's head spin, and suddenly Martin again experienced a feeling he had known on more than one occasion as a child: an unbearable intensification of all his senses, a magical and demanding impulse, the presence of something for which alone it was worth living."

—From chapter 5 of Nabokov's fifth novel, *Glory* (1932)

★ ★ ★ ★ ★ ★ ★ ★

"I was born in a land where the idea of freedom, the notion of right, the habit of human kindness were things coldly despised and brutally outlawed. Now and then, in the course of history, a hypocrite government would paint the walls of the nation's prison a comelier shade of yellow and loudly proclaim the granting of rights familiar to happier states; but either these rights were solely enjoyed by the jailers or else they contained some secret flaw which made them even more bitter than the decrees of frank tyranny... From time to time a thing called revolution would occur, turning the slaves into bullies and vice versa ... A dark country, a hellish place, gentlemen, and if there is anything *of which I am certain in life it is that I shall never exchange the liberty of my exile for the vile parody of home . . ."*—From "The Doubtful Asphodel," by Sebastian Knight, one of the novels within Nabokov's novel *The Real Life of Sebastian Knight*, which was his first book written in English (while living in France, 1937-1940; published in U.S. and England, 1941, by New Directions)

"As I look back at those years of exile, I see myself, and thousands of other Russians, leading an odd but by no means unpleasant existence, in material indigence and intellectual luxury, among perfectly unimportant strangers, spectral Germans and Frenchmen in whose more or less illusory cities we, émigrés, happened to dwell. These aborigines were to the mind's eye as flat and transparent as figures cut out of cellophane, and although we used their gadgets, applauded their clowns, picked their roadside plums and apples, no real communication, of the rich human sort so widespread in our own midst, existed between us and them. It seemed at times that we ignored them the way an arrogant or very stupid invader ignores a formless and faceless mass of natives; but occasionally, quite often in fact, the spectral world through which we serenely paraded our sores and our arts would produce a kind of awful convulsion and show us who was the discarnate captive and who the true lord. Our utter physical dependence on this or that nation, which had coldly granted us political refuge, became painfully evident when some trashy 'visa,' some diabolical 'identity card' had to be obtained or prolonged, for then an avid bureaucratic hell would attempt to close upon the petitioner and he might wilt while his dossier waxed fatter and fatter in the desks of rat-whiskered consuls and policemen. Dokumenti, *it has been said, is a Russian's placenta. The League of Nations equipped émigrés who had lost their Russian citizenship with a so-called 'Nansen' passport, a very inferior document of a sickly green hue. Its holder was little better than a criminal on parole and had to go through most hideous ordeals every time he wished to travel from one country to another, and the smaller the countries the worse the fuss they made. Somewhere at the back of their glands, the authorities secreted the notion that no matter how bad a state—say, Soviet Russia—might be, any fugitive from it was intrinsically despicable since he existed outside a national administration; and therefore he was viewed with the preposterous disapproval with which certain religious groups regard a child born out of wedlock. Not all of us consented to be bastards and ghosts. Sweet are the recollections some Russian émigrés treasure of how they insulted or fooled high officials at various ministries,* Préfectures *and* Polizeipraesidiums.

" . . . Today, in a new and beloved world, where I have learned to

feel at home as easily as I have ceased barring my sevens, extroverts and cosmopolitans to whom I happen to mention these past matters think I am jesting, or accuse me of snobbery in reverse, when I maintain that in the course of almost one-fifth of a century spent in Western Europe I have not had, among the sprinklings of Germans and Frenchmen I knew (mostly landladies and literary people), more than two good friends all told." —From chapter 14 of *Speak, Memory* (which is a revised and expanded version of a memoir called *Conclusive Evidence*, which Nabokov published in 1951, while living in America)

* * * * * * * *

"The story of my college years in England is really the story of my trying to become a Russian writer. I had the feeling that Cambridge and all its famed features—venerable elms, blazoned windows, loquacious tower clocks—were of no consequence in themselves but existed merely to frame and support my rich nostalgia . . . My fear of losing or corrupting, through alien influence, the only thing I had salvaged from Russia—her language—became positively morbid and considerably more harassing than the fear I was to experience two decades later of my never being able to bring my English prose anywhere close to the level of my Russian."

—From Chapter 13 of *Speak, Memory*

In 1921, Nabokov filed this dispatch to the Russian-language émigré newspaper *The Rudder*, which his father V. D. Nabokov had co-founded in Berlin: *"I sometimes sit in a corner and look about me at all these smooth faces, very attractive, one has to grant, but somehow always calling to mind advertisements for shaving cream, and suddenly it becomes so boring, so tedious that you almost want to whoop and smash some windows. . . .*

"We Russians and they have a certain glass wall between us; they have their own worlds, round and hard, like a painstakingly painted globe. Their souls do not know that whirlwind of inspiration, pulsation, radiance, that furious dance, that malevolence and tenderness, which transport us into God-only-knows-what heavens and abysses; we have moments when the clouds are about our shoulders and the sea about our knees—go free, my soul! For an Englishman this is incomprehensible, unheard of, yes, and alluring. If, having had a bit to drink, he does cause an uproar, that uproar is stereotyped and good-natured, and the guardians of order only smile as they watch him, knowing that he will not go beyond a certain point. Or, to put it another way, even the most furious drunkenness will not cause him to be deeply

stirred, to bare his chest, to hurl his cap against the earth."

★ ★ ★ ★ ★ ★ ★ ★

"Q: What are your views about man's upward climb from slime?
"A: 'A truly remarkable performance. Pity, though, that some of the slime still sticks to drugged brains.'— Interviewed by Israel Shenker, The New York *Times Book Review,* January 9, 1972

ON THE EVENTS OF MARCH 28, 1922: "The fullest account of the assassination of V. D. Nabokov is, for obvious reasons, to be found in the pages of *The Rudder*. It occurred at a political evening at the Berlin Philharmonic Hall. Nabokov was to introduce his Kadet adversary, Pavel Miliukov, and there was hope that the breach between them which had progressively widened since 1920 was to be healed on this evening, as, in a grim way, it was. Two right-wing extremists named Shabelsky and Taboritsky, living in Munich, read of the evening and traveled to Berlin with the express purpose of assassinating Miliukov, whom the monarchists held to be indirectly responsible for the murder of Nicholas II by the Bolsheviks. (Miliukov had publicly taken the position that monarchy was no longer necessary in Russia.) Shabelsky and Taboritsky rose from their seats in the second row, guns in hand, and headed straight for the dais. Amid great uproar and confusion, as Shabelsky aimed his gun at Miliukov, Nabokov lunged between them, deflecting the assassin's hand and receiving a bullet slightly below the heart. In the meantime, Taboritsky jumped onto the stage and began to wave his pistol and shout melodramatically until he was tackled, but not before he had had a chance to fire at Nabokov's prostrate body. In all, Nabokov was shot three times, and it was never made entirely clear which of the assassins had actually killed him. Nabokov's son, then a student at Cambridge, was in Berlin at that time, but he was not at the meeting and received the news at home by telephone and arrived at the hall some minutes later.

"A certain air of mystery and confusion hangs over the entire crime, and reading the accounts of the interrogation and trial of the two killers (one of whom was to attain a position of some importance under Hitler in later years) one gets a glimmer of what might have happened had Lee Harvey Oswald lived . . ."
—Andrew Field in *Nabokov: His Life in Art* (1967)

"Oh, how did he die? From illness? From exposure? From thirst? By

the hand of man? And if—by somebody's hand, can that hand be still living, taking bread, raising a glass, chasing flies, stirring, pointing, beckoning, lying motionless, shaking other hands? Did he return their fire for a long time? Did he save a last bullet for himself? Was he taken alive? Did they bring him to the parlor car at the railway headquarters of some punitive detachment (I can see its hideous locomotive stoked with dried fish), having suspected him of being a White spy . . .? Did they shoot him in the ladies' room of some godforsaken station (broken looking glass, tattered plush), or did they lead him out into some kitchen garden one dark night and wait for the moon to peep out? How did he wait for them in the dark? With a smile of disdain?

—Fyodor on his father in *The Gift,* Nabokov's last novel in Russian (written 1935-1937, partially serialized 1937-1938, published in book form in Russian, 1952, in English, 1963)

"One has only to recall how much Dostoevsky's critics and biographers have made of *his* father's violent death to realize that Nabokov's art can scarcely hope to escape the same fate. Certainly the assassination by mistake in *Pale Fire* recalls the circumstances in which Nabokov's father died, and one could fill several pages with a list of violent deaths and appearances of guns in Nabokov's writing . . . Nabokov has said that he is certain that Shabelsky and Taboritsky have never entered his art, and perhaps this is so, if they are seen as merely another variation—and a particularly stupid one—on the violence that has been the lot of almost all Russians in this century. The Russian police state, Nabokov has acknowledged, is always at the back of his emigre mind."

—Andrew Field in *Nabokov: His Life in Art*

"But careful: I like to recall what my father wrote: 'When closely— no matter how closely—observing events in nature we must, in the very process of observation, beware of letting our reason—that garrulous dragoman who always runs ahead—prompt us with explanations which then begin imperceptibly to influence the very course of observation and distort it: thus the shadow of the instrument falls upon the truth.' "—The Gift. "Dragoman" is an Eastern term for a professional interpreter.

* * * * * * *

ANYA IN WONDERLAND

"In the Russian version of his autobiography, Vladimir Nabokov tells us that he translated *Alice in Wonderland* into Russian during his free-lancing days after returning to Berlin from his studies at

Cambridge and that he was paid the sum of five American dollars for the job. In both of the English versions of the autobiography *(Conclusive Evidence* and *Speak, Memory),* he supplies the additional information that five dollars was 'quite a sum during the inflation in Germany.' The translation, signed with the pen-name Nabokov used during his European period, V. Sirin, was brought out in Berlin in 1923 by an émigré publishing house named after the legendary bird of Russian mythology, Gamaiun. . . .

"Beyond his success with parodies and puns, Nabokov's version of Carroll is remarkable for its beautifully caught and conveyed tone and diction of the original. If it is not the perfect translation it could have been, it is because it does contain pages not equal in imagination and fidelity to what Nabokov has done in the best and most successful passages. *Anya in Wonderland,* we must remember, was translated by a very young man, working for money and possibly trying to meet a deadline. Still, with a few subsequent revisions, the book could have easily become one of the finest translations of *Alice* into any language. Even without these revisions, it is by far the best one that exists in Russian. And yet, apart from a few copies in the largest libraries of the Western world, it is also one of the least available versions of *Alice."*

—Simon Karlinsky in *TriQuarterly*
(winter, 1970)

* * * * * * * *

"Yasha and I had entered Berlin University at almost exactly the same time, but I did not know him although we must have passed each other many times. Diversity of subjects . . . diminished the possibility of our association. If I were to return now into that past, enriched in but one respect—awareness of the present day—and retrace exactly all my interlooping steps, then I would certainly notice his face, now so familiar to me through snapshots. It is a funny thing, when you imagine yourself returning into the past with the contraband of the present, how weird it would be to encounter there, in unexpected places, the prototypes of today's acquaintances, so young and fresh, who in a kind of lucid lunacy do not recognize you; thus a woman, for instance, whom one loves since yesterday, appears as a young girl, standing practically next to one in a crowded train, while the chance passerby who fifteen years ago asked you the way in the street now works in the same office as you." —*The Gift*

* * * * * * * *

NABOKOV IN THE THIRTIES:

"I knew him well in the thirties when he began to visit Paris (from Berlin) and when, finally, before the war, he settled there with his wife and son. I gradually got used to his manner (not acquired in the U.S.A., but always there) of not recognizing people, of addressing Ivan Ivanovich, after knowing him many years, as 'Ivan Petrovich,' of calling Nina Nikolaevna 'Nina Aleksandrovna,' the book of verse *In the West [Na Zapade]* 'On One's Ass' ["Na Zadnitse"], of washing from the face of the earth someone who had been kind to him, of mocking in print a man kindly disposed to him (as in his review of Aldanov's *The Cave*), of taking something from a great author and then saying he had never read him. I know all that now; here, however, I am discussing not him but his books. I stand at the 'dusty crossroads' and look at his 'royal procession' with thanks and the awareness that my generation (including of course myself) will live in him, that it did not disappear, did not dissolve itself between the Billancourt cemetery, Shanghai, New York, and Prague. All of us, with our entire weight, be we successful (if there are such) or unsuccessful (a round dozen), rest on him. *If Nabokov is alive, it means that I am as well!*"—Nina Berberova of Princeton's Slavic department in *TriQuarterly* (winter, 1970). Her closing line echoes Tolstoy's, in "Master and Man,": *"Zhiv Nikita, znachit zhiv i ya!"* Billancourt, in France, was where Nabokov visited the major Russian émigré poet and literary critic Vladisha Khodasevich, whose 1937 essay, "On Sirin," consolidated Nabokov's reputation as the emigration's most accomplished writer. Nabokov's subsequent novel, *The Gift*, contains a remarkable imaginary conversation with Khodasevich (therein called Koncheyev), which actually, according to Nina Berberova, took place in 1932 at Billancourt. Khodasevich died in 1939 and, almost a quarter of a century later, in his foreword to *The Gift*, Nabokov hailed Khodasevich as "the greatest Russian poet that the twentieth century has yet produced."

NABOKOV IN PARIS, 1937-1940:

"Volodia [diminutive for Vladimir] and his family had found a flat in the rue Boileau in Auteuil, a residential section of Paris. Almost every Russian loves living in France, however hard his material circumstances might be . . . But Volodia simply could not acclimate himself to the French way of life. To us the family appeared profoundly miserable for the entire period of their Paris sojourn. It was with the greatest joy that they received all necessary permits and papers enabling them to leave for the United States, thus escaping the war and the ensuing debacle, the Fall of France. In America they found a new home and once again Nabokov enjoyed working

. . .

"One day in 1938 Volodia asked me whether I would like to go over his first manuscript in English, a novel he had written in the small bathroom of their apartment. It was entitled *The Real Life of Sebastian Knight*. I was of course delighted at his suggestion

. . .

"So Volodia started coming over several afternoons a week, around 3 P.M. He was always on time. He was most anxious that this first novel in English should sound neither 'foreign' nor read as though it had been translated into English. We both sat at the large mahogany desk and worked for several hours each time. I would read out a sentence and see how it sounded. Most of it read amazingly smoothly. Occasionally a word had to be changed, or a more suitable synonym sought. Sometimes one word was better than two. We would argue the point, and I might delete my suggestion, or he would capitulate. He would then read it out again, in his deep baritone, and I would listen. We had a little trouble with certain passages, but the author knew exactly the manner in which he wished to convey his thought. With most passages we had no trouble at all."—Lucie Léon Noel in *TriQuarterly* (winter, 1970). It was at the Paris home of Mrs. Noel and her husband, Paul, that Nabokov met James Joyce, but neither Nabokov nor his hostess could remember anything that was said.

NABOKOV vs SARTRE:

When Nabokov's 1936 Russian novel, *Despair,* was published in French in 1939, Jean-Paul Sartre reviewed it thusly:
"It seems to me that this desperate eagerness to attack and destroy himself is quite characteristic of the manner of M. Nabokov. This author has a great deal of talent, but it is of the old school. I am thinking of his spiritual mentors, particularly Dostoevsky. . . . But Dostoevsky believed in his characters. M. Nabokov no longer believes in his, nor even in the art of the novel. He does not conceal borrowing Dostoevsky's artistic method, even as he ridicules it.

. . .

Here, one thinks in closing the book, is a lot of noise for nothing."
Ten years later, Nabokov reviewed the English translation of

Sartre's first novel in the New York *Times Book Review* (April 24, 1949):

"Nausea *belongs to that tense-looking but really very loose type of writing, which has been popularized by many second-raters—Barbusse, Celine, and so forth. Somewhere behind looms Dostoevsky at his worst, and still farther back there is old Eugene Sue, to whom the melodramatic Russian owed so much. . . . But the task to make the world exist as a work of art was beyond Sartre's powers."*

Sixteen years thereafter, Nabokov still was not done with roasting Sartre. In his 1965 preface to the American edition of *Despair*, Nabokov noted that it *"has less White-Russian appeal than have my other emigre novels; hence it will be less puzzling and irritating to those readers who have been brought up on the leftist propaganda of the thirties."* Wedged inside that sentence, next to its semicolon, was an asterisk that led to a footnote: *"This did not prevent a Communist reviewer (J. P. Sartre), who devoted in 1939 a remarkably silly article to the French translation of* Despair, *from saying that 'both the author and the main character are the victims of the war and the emigration.'"*

Andrew Field writes, in *Nabokov: His Life in Art:*

"Sartre's essay on Nabokov is perhaps the most intellectually careless thing ever written by him, and it is worth quoting . . . both because Sartre subsequently deemed it worth reprinting and because it serves as a splendidly low watermark in the critical literature on Nabokov and on Russian émigré writing in general. . . .

"*Despair* is, measured against the outstanding fiction of this century, a major novel—the first one Nabokov wrote—but it has been its poor fortune to be overshadowed by some four or five other later Nabokov novels . . . It should properly be compared not with *Lolita, The Gift,* and *Pale Fire,* but with the best works of Fitzgerald, Waugh, Anderson, Faulkner, and Hemingway (choose any two)."

★ ★ ★ ★ ★ ★ ★ ★

"*The first little throb of* Lolita *went through me late in 1939 or early in 1940, in Paris, at a time when I was laid up with a severe attack of intercostal neuralgia. As far as I can recall, the initial shiver of inspiration was somehow prompted by a newspaper story about an ape in the Jardin des Plantes, who, after months of coaxing by a scientist, produced the first drawing ever charcoaled by an animal: this sketch showed the bars of the poor creature's cage. The impulse I record had no textual connection with the ensuing train of thought, which result-*

ed, however, in a prototype of my present novel, a short story some thirty pages long. I wrote it in Russian. . . . The man was a Central European, the anonymous nymphet was French, and the loci were Paris and Provence. I had him marry the little girl's sick mother who soon died, and after a thwarted attempt to take advantage of the orphan in a hotel room, Arthur (for that was his name) threw himself under the wheels of a truck. I read the story one blue-papered wartime night to a group of friends—Mark Aldanov, two social revolutionaries, and a woman doctor; but I was not pleased with the thing and destroyed it sometime after moving to America in 1940."—From "On a Book Entitled *LOLITA*," written in 1956 for *The Anchor Review*, which published it in 1957; later it was appended to the 1958 Putnam edition of *Lolita* as an afterword.

But in *The Gift*, the novel which Nabokov wrote in Russian between 1935 and 1937, an émigré landlord in Berlin tells writer Fyodor:
"Ah, if only I had a tick or two, what a novel I'd whip off! From real life. Imagine this kind of thing: an old dog—but still in his prime, fiery, thirsting for happiness—gets to know a widow, and she has a daughter, still quite a little girl—you know what I mean—when nothing is formed yet but already she has a way of walking that drives you out of your mind—A slip of a girl, very fair, pale, with blue under the eyes—and of course she doesn't even look at the old goat. What to do? Well, not long thinking, he ups and marries the widow. Okay. They settle down the three of them. Here you can go on indefinitely—the temptation, the eternal torment, the itch, the mad hopes. And the upshot—a miscalculation. Time flies, he gets older, she blossoms out—and not a sausage. Just walks by and scorches you with a look of contempt. Eh? D'you feel a kind of Dostoevskian tragedy? That story, you see, happened to a great friend of mine, once upon a time in fairyland when Old King Cole was a merry old soul."

★ ★ ★ ★ ★ ★ ★ ★

INTERVIEW WITH A DICTATOR:
" 'If,' said Krug, 'you cannot leave me and my friends in peace, then let them and me go abroad. It would save you a world of trouble.
" 'What is it exactly you have against my government?'
" 'I am not in the least interested in your government. What I resent is your attempt to make me interested in it. Leave me alone.'
" 'Alone' is the vilest word in the language. Nobody is alone. When a cell in an organism says "leave me alone," the result is cancer.' "
—from Nabokov's first "American" novel, *Bend Sinister* (1947)

"Nabokov has called himself an 'American writer, born in Russia and educated in England where I studied French literature, before spending fifteen years in Germany.' The particular quality of Nabokov's Americanism is captured by the thing he first admired about Americans when he arrived in the United States: the way they held their hands in their pockets."—Andrew Field in *Nabokov: His Life in Art*

"*I hope to write some day a 'Speak on, Memory,' covering the years 1940-60 spent in America: the evaporation of certain volatiles and the melting of certain metals are still going on in my coils and crucibles.*"— From 1966 foreword to *Speak, Memory*

NABOKOV AT WELLESLEY, 1941-1948:

"*As a teacher, Nabokov was provocative, tough, highhanded. At Wellesley, anxious to get off on a June butterfly hunt, he startled the registrar's office by wanting to turn in his grades before the final exam. He already knew, he said, exactly what each of his students was worth. When he did give an exam, it was demanding. Appalled by the constant cheating, he browbeat students to go to the toilet before the papers were passed out and pressed fresh pencils into the hands of examinees rather than let them go to the sharpener.*" —from *Time* cover story, May 23, 1969

> "*The rhyme is the line's birthday, as you know,
> and there are certain customary twins
> in Russian as in other tongues. For instance,
> love automatically rhymes with blood,
> nature with liberty, sadness with distance,
> humane with everlasting, prince with mud,
> moon with a multitude of words, but sun
> and song and wind and life and death with none.*"
> —Stanza of 1945 poem, "An Evening of Russian Poetry"

NABOKOV AT CORNELL, 1948-1959:

'By the way,' he explained in casual audacity, seeming to exaggerate his Russian accent to heighten the effect, 'Joyce made only one error in English usage in *Ulysses*, the use of "supine" instead of "prone."'

" 'Art is useful only when it is futile,' he would read (but he was such a superb actor, one of the basic requirements of a 'great teacher,' that no one knew he wrote out his lectures, word for word, down to the wryest 'asides'). 'The artist is a sublime liar. . . . Art is not *about* something but it is the thing itself. . . . Art is not a simple arithmetic but a delicate calculus. . . . In art, the roundabout hits the center. . . . Life is the least realistic of fictions . . .

" 'There are two million words in this course,' Nabokov would say, explaining that the novels added up to a million words but that we were to read them—'every single one of them'—twice, the first time merely to get such trivial concerns as 'plot suspense' out of the way. I recall a comparison to painting—one should approach a novel as one approaches a painting, not going from left to right but taking in the whole, a simultaneous totality of experience. But just to make sure, he made a point of giving away the plots in the first lecture so that the poshlosts among us. . . .

"Poshlost? He would look up, mimicking surprise that we didn't know the word, then explain that it was a peculiarly Russian word (as untranslatable as 'corny,' with as many specific instances and as little specific meaning as 'camp'), a kind of subtle vulgarity, not crude or coarse, but verging on sensitivity, sensitivity with a slight tinge of mold—Olivier's *Hamlet,* for instance, with its 'Freudian staircases,' or 'the great ideas,' or the novels of Thomas Mann. . . .

"Nabokov was a great teacher not because he taught the subject well but because he exemplified, and stimulated in his students, a profound and loving attitude toward it. Of course his eccentric personality intrigued us (as a matter of fact, he was considered a kind of Pnin-figure), but his vivid enthusiasms entranced us, and we emerged from his course not so much 'educated' as transfigured. Nabokov didn't 'teach' novels, he gazed at them with such joyful and tender devotion that they became for us what they already were for him—'shimmering prisms.'
—Ross Wetzsteon in *The Village Voice*

"As a lecturer, Nabokov was a considerable Thespian, able to manipulate audiences in a similar manner. His rehearsal of Gogol's death agonies remains in one's mind: how the hack doctors alternately bled him and purged him and plunged him into icy baths, Gogol so frail that his spine could be felt through his stomach, the six fat white bloodletting leeches clinging to his nose, Gogol begging to have them removed—*'Please lift them, lift them, lift them, keep them away!'*—and, sinking behind the lectern, now a tub, Nabokov for several moments *was* Gogol, shuddering and shivering, his hands held down by a husky attendant, his head thrown back in pain and terror, nostrils distended, eyes shut, his beseechments filling the large lecture hall. Even the sea of C-minuses in the back of the room could not help being moved.

And then, after a pause, Nabokov would very quietly say, in a sentence taken word-for-word from his *Gogol*, 'Although the scene is unpleasant and has a human appeal which I deplore, it is necessary to dwell upon it a little longer in order to bring out the curiously physical side of Gogol's genius.' "—Alfred Appel, Jr., in his introduction to *The Annotated LOLITA* (1970)

"*I loved teaching. I loved Cornell. I loved composing and delivering my lectures on Russian writers and European great books. But around 60, and especially in winter, one begins to find hard the physical process of teaching, the getting up at a fixed hour every other morning, the struggle with the snow in the driveway, the march through long corridors to the classroom, the effort of drawing on the blackboard a map of James Joyce's Dublin or the arrangement of the semi-sleeping car of the St. Petersburg-Moscow express in the early 1870's—without an understanding of which neither* Ulysses *nor* Anna Karenina*, respectively, makes sense. For some reason my most vivid memories concern examinations. Big amphitheater in Goldwin Smith. Exams from 8 A.M. to 10:30. About 150 students—unwashed, unshaven young males and reasonably well-groomed young females. A general sense of tedium and disaster. Half-past eight. Little coughs, the clearing of nervous throats, coming in clusters of sound, rustling of pages. Some of the martyrs plunged in meditation, their arms locked behind their heads. I meet a dull gaze directed at me, seeing in me with hope and hate the source of forbidden knowledge. Girl in glasses comes up to my desk to ask: 'Professor Kafka, do you want us to say that . . .? Or do you want us to answer only the first part of the question?' The great fraternity of C-minus, backbone of the nation, steadily scribbling on. A rustle arising simultaneously, the majority turning a page in their bluebooks, good teamwork. The shaking of a cramped wrist, the failing ink, the deodorant that breaks down. When I catch eyes directed at me, they are forthwith raised to the ceiling in pious meditation. Windowpanes getting misty. Boys peeling off sweaters. Girls chewing gum in rapid cadence. Ten minutes, five, three, time's up.*"
—In *Playboy* interview, 1964

* * * * * * * *

"*Do you recognize that clover?*
Dandelions, l'or du pauvre?
(Europe, nonetheless, is over)."
—stanza of 1953 poem, "Lines Written in Oregon"

"*Lolita, light of my life, fire of my loins. My sin, my soul, Lo-lee-ta:*

the tip of the tongue taking a trip of three steps down the palate to tap, at three, on the teeth. Lo. Lee. Ta.
"*She was Lo, plain Lo, in the morning, standing four feet ten in one sock. She was Lola in slacks. She was Dolly at school. She was Dolores on the dotted line. But in my arms she was always Lolita.*"
—Opening passage of *Lolita*

"As might be expected . . . the history of *LOLITA* since it first appeared in an edition issued by the Olympia Press of Paris in 1955 has been a fascinating one. Only now, three years after original publication, is an American edition being published, but it has been or is being translated into Danish, Swedish, French, Italian, German and Dutch. In the interim the original English edition was banned in France by the French Government, apparently as the result of pressure from the British Home Secretary, although the United States Customs Office found the book unobjectionable and permitted its importation into this country." —From the jacket of the 1958 Putnam edition

Brock Brower writes: "My own copy of *Lolita* happens to come not late from G. P. Putnam's Sons but early from the Olympia Press. The two-volume, sewer-green-covered 1955 edition with its quick-rot, slime binding and its heavy pollution of typos. That is the actual, physical feel of the book—much as *Ada,* at the other end of the scale, now has the black, basaltic weight in my hand of an encyclopedist's tombstone—and I mention this very minor fact of sensation to recall a time, a now forgotten time in Nabokov's career when he was struggling to gain recognition for *Lolita* above the pornography line, and when we, his avid readers, had no end of difficulty simply getting hold of a copy."

Brower and his wife, then living in New York, borrowed a copy that was available for one night only: "We tried, but *Lolita* is not the kind of book that somebody can read hastily overnight, particularly both somebodies. We had to send instead to a friend in Paris. The friend wrote us later that she'd gone promptly to Brentano's with our under-the-counter order, but in that case she was unconscionably late in forwarding the contraband. It finally arrived, much thumbed through, obviously several times read, and under cover—another ironic comment, I think, on Nabokov's *émigré* status—of a UNESCO envelope."
—*TriQuarterly* (winter, 1970)

Two poets discussing *Lolita* on a farm in Kirchstetten, Austria, spring of 1971:

WYSTAN HUGH AUDEN: It's not in the least pornographic. It's a very funny book of anagrams."
CHESTER SIMON KALLMAN: "It's a very sad book."
W.H.A.: "But there are no scenes in it that are pornographic."
C.S.K.: "Oh, well, Wystan, there *are*."
W.H.A.: "No, not really. It's all a game of words."
—From *W.H. Auden: In the Autumn of the Age of Anxiety*

"Now I wish to introduce the following idea. Between the age limits of nine and fourteen there occur maidens who, to certain bewitched travelers, twice or many times older than they, reveal their true nature, which is not human, but nymphic (that is, demoniac); and these chosen creatures I propose to designate as 'nymphets.'

"It will be marked that I substitute time terms for spatial ones. In fact, I would have the reader see 'nine' and 'fourteen' as the boundaries—the mirrory beaches and rosy rocks—of an enchanted island haunted by those nymphets of mine and surrounded by a vast, misty sea. Between those age limits, are all girl-children nymphets? Of course not. Otherwise, we who are in the know, we lone voyagers, we nympholepts, would have long gone insane. Neither are good looks any criterion.... A normal man given a group photograph of school girls or Girl Scouts and asked to point out the comeliest one will not necessarily choose the nymphet among them. You have to be an artist and a madman, a creature of infinite melancholy, with a bubble of hot poison in your loins and a super-voluptuous flame permanently aglow in your subtle spine (oh, how you have to cringe and hide!), in order to discern at once, by ineffable signs—the slightly feline outline of a cheekbone, the slenderness of a downy limb, and other indices which despair and shame and tears of tenderness forbid me to tabulate—the little deadly demon among the wholesome children; she *stands unrecognized by them and unconscious herself of her fantastic power.*"

—From part 1, chapter 5 of *Lolita*

"Much of the humor of *Lolita* results from shock. It is perfectly outrageous for Humbert to be so blithe about his sexual relationship with a child. We are shocked by, but at the same time must laugh at, his clinical exposition of the affair. Humbert is mad, but if one accepts his premises it is the world around him that is mad. ... Rarely does a novel demand so liberal a mind of its readers—and certainly there are literate people who find *Lolita* offensive. There will be some who will find it subversive of American morality. Already someone has seen it as an allegorical seducing of the New World by the Old. But there will be a few who will see that Nabokov has written nothing more or less than an American *Dead Souls.*"—From "A Review of a Novel You Can't Buy," by Richard Schickel, in *The Reporter,* November 28, 1957

"*Lolita* is a novel of prisons. Humbert Humbert is in prison as he writes the book. Lolita herself, most obviously, was Humbert's prisoner, but he, too, was hers, as, in quite a different way, he was also the prisoner of Lolita's mother Charlotte during their brief marriage. Beneath the neon smiles of their vacancy signs, the motels at which Humbert and Lolita stay in their flight across America are transient prisons: 'WE WISH YOU TO FEEL AT HOME WHILE HERE. ALL EQUIPMENT WAS CAREFULLY CHECKED UPON YOUR ARRIVAL. YOUR LICENSE NUMBER IS ON RECORD HERE. USE HOT WATER SPARINGLY. WE RESERVE THE RIGHT TO EJECT WITHOUT NOTICE ANY OBJECTIONABLE PERSON.' Most of all, Humbert is a prisoner of his past, the idyllic and brutally disrupted childhood romance which he is sentenced to attempt to repeat in his grotesque longing for nymphets. Nymphets themselves are eventually imprisoned in the excessive flesh of maturity ('the coffin of coarse female flesh in which my nymphets are buried alive'). When Lolita escapes (is kidnapped) from Humbert with Quilty, it is because she has been momentarily transferred from the captivity of Humbert to that of a provincial American hospital where she is guarded from him by an imperious young nurse. And at the end of the novel Humbert imprisons and executes Quilty in his own house, after having carefully removed all the keys from the doors beforehand so that the prisoner cannot lock himself away from his executioner."—Andrew Field in *Nabokov: His Life in Art (1967)*

"Alas, I was unable to transcend the simple human fact that . . . nothing could make my Lolita forget the foul lust I had inflicted upon her. Unless it can be proven to me—to me as I am now, today, with my heart and my beard, and my putrefaction—that in the infinite run it does not matter a jot that a North American girl-child named Dolores Haze had been deprived of her childhood by a maniac, unless this can be proven (and it it can, then life is a joke), I see nothing for the treatment of my misery but the melancholy and very local palliative of articulate art."

—from part 2, chapter 31 of *Lolita*

"The fact that Lolita was never brought before the courts at all in this country, as she was in England, has tended to obscure this eccentric (as usual) Nabokovian effect on literary censorship. The case of *Ulysses* came long before, and those of *Lady Chatterley's Lover, Tropic of Cancer,* and *Fanny Hill* came almost too quickly thereafter. But the avoidance of any attack upon *Lolita* is, I suspect, the secret turning point. And I don't think this inaction came only because of the book's obvious 'redeeming' literary qualities. It occurred equally because *Lolita* was uneasily understood, recognized in some unconscious way, as a prophetic work.

"Prophetic in a quite literal sense. To read her sad history now . . . is to catch an agonizing glimpse of present-day America in pupa. The motel culture, the coming of the teeny-bopper, our endless mobility, the malaise of sexual freedom, the corrupt beauty of plastic, even the fashion of violence are all there in the brilliant haze of this iridescent comedy."

—Brock Brower in *TriQuarterly* (winter, 1970)

"There are gentle souls who would pronounce Lolita *meaningless because it does not teach them anything. I am neither a reader nor a writer of didactic fiction, and, despite John Ray's assertion,* Lolita *has no moral in tow. For me a work of fiction exists only insofar as it affords me what I shall bluntly call aesthetic bliss, that is a sense of being somehow, somewhere connected with other states of being where art (curiosity, tenderness, kindness, ecstasy) is the norm. There are not many such books. All the rest is either topical trash or what some call the Literature of Ideas, which very often is topical trash coming in huge blocks of plaster that are carefully transmitted from age to age until somebody comes along with a hammer and takes a good crack at Balzac, at Gorki, at Mann."*

—From the afterword, "On a Book Entitled *Lolita*"

★ ★ ★ ★ ★ ★ ★ ★

"Now I shall speak of evil as none has
Spoken before. I loathe such things as jazz;
The white-hosed moron torturing a black
Bull, rayed with red; abstractist bric-a-brac;
Primitivist folk-masks; progressive schools;
Music in supermarkets; swimming pools;
Brutes, bores, class-conscious Philistines, Freud-Marx,
Fake thinkers, puffed-up poets, frauds and sharks."

—Lines 923-930 of John Shade's poem, "Pale Fire," in the novel *Pale Fire,* (1962)

In Charles Kinbote's "Commentary" to the poem "Pale Fire," his

notes on line 922 conclude:
"*After this line, instead of 923-930, we find the following, lightly deleted, variant:*
"*All artists have been born in what they call
a sorry age; mine is the worst of all:
An age that thinks spacebombs and spaceships take
A genius with a foreign name to make,
When any jackass can rig up the stuff;
An age in which a pack of rogues can bluff
The selenographer; a comic age
That sees in Dr. Schweitzer a great sage.*

"*Having struck this out, the poet tried another theme, but those lines he also canceled:*
"*England where poets flew the highest, now
Wants them to plod and Pegasus to plough;
Now the prosemongers of the Grubby Group,
The Message Man, the owlish Nincompoop
And all the Social Novels of our age
Leave but a pinch of coal dust on the page.*"

"Above Shade and Kinbote, the poem and the Commentary is Nabokov himself, who is the most important of the three artists, and who imposes his own pattern upon *Pale Fire* without in any way impinging upon the separate designs of the poet Shade and the madman-artist he has created. This aspect of the novel is clearest and most serenely open and obvious when seen in the perspective of Nabokov's entire artistic career. . . . I think it safe to say that there might have been a good deal less bafflement over *Pale Fire* if such earlier Russian Nabokov novels as *The Defense* and *The Gift* had been translated into English prior to 1962; and there would beyond any doubt have been a great deal less if some of the articles by Nabokov's best Russian critic, Vladislav Khodasevich, had appeared in English translation. It was Khodasevich who very early in Nabokov's writing career declared that his sole thematic concern is art, and that he writes only about artists—failed artists, aspiring artists, mad artists, every conceivable kind of artist—but that he does this in allegorical form, choosing as his protagonists chess players, homosexuals and murderers. I would have the reader of Nabokov always bear in mind this wise and simple observation—though it doesn't *always* apply."
—Andrew Field in *TriQuarterly* (winter, 1967)

"*My second wand-stroke is this: among the many gifts I showered on Martin, I was careful not to include talent. How easy it would have been to make him an artist, a writer; how hard not to let him be one, while bestowing on him the keen sensitivity that one generally associates with the creative creature; how cruel to prevent him from finding in art—not an "escape" (which is only a cleaner cell on a quieter floor), but relief from the itch of being! The temptation to perform my own little exploit within the omnibus nimbus prevailed."*

—From foreword in late 1970 to 1971 English translation of 1932 novel, *Glory*

"... *Lolita* in due course was recognized as the masterpiece it is, and it made Nabokov rich, setting him free for the first time in his life, at 59, to write full time.

"The first fruit of that freedom was *Pale Fire*. Spectacularly unread, it made no concessions to popular tastes while proving that a genius can write a brilliant novel consisting of a 999-line poem and scholarly comment on it. The book is a wintry, touching parable concerning two of Nabokov's persistent themes—the feeling of being unloved and the horror of willfully inflicted pain. *Pale Fire* elicited the high-water mark of Nabokov's critical acceptance."

— *Time* cover story, May 23, 1969

* * * * * * * *

"I have never been interested in what is called the literature of social comment (in journalistic and commercial parlance: 'great books.') I am not 'sincere,' I am not 'provocative,' I am not 'satirical.' I am neither a didacticist nor an allegorizer. Politics and economics, atomic bombs, primitive and abstract art forms, the entire Orient, symptoms of 'thaw' in Soviet Russia, the Future of Mankind, and so on, leave me supremely indifferent. As in the case of my Invitation to a Beheading ... *automatic comparisons between* Bend Sinister *and Kafka's creations or Orwell's clichés would go merely to prove that the automaton could not have read either the great German writer or the mediocre English one."*

—*Introduction to 1965 Time-Life* Books edition of a volume in the *Time* Reading Program of *Bend Sinister* (1947)

"Speaking in a curiously ornate and literary English lightly tinctured with a Russian accent, choosing his words with self-conscious deliberation, he seemed somewhat dubious of his ability to make himself understood—or perhaps skeptical about the advisability of doing so. Despite the good humor and well-bred cordiality which marked our meetings, it was as though the shad-

owed universe within his skull was forever beckoning him away from a potentially hostile world outside. Thus his conversation, like his fiction—in which so many critics have sought vainly to unearth autobiography—veils rather than reveals the man; and he seems to prefer it that way."
    —Alvin Toffler's introduction to his *Playboy* interview with Nabokov (1964)

"His works are an edifice whose every corner rewards inspection. Each book, including the super-slim *Poems* and the uproariously pedantic and copious commentaries to his translation of *Eugene Onegin,* yields delight and presents to the aesthetic sense the peculiar hardness of a finished, fully meant thing. His sentences are beautiful out of context and doubly beautiful in it. He writes prose the only way it should be written—that is, ecstatically. In the intensity of its intelligence and reflective joy, his fiction is unique in this decade and scarcely precedented in American literature."
—From John Updike's review of *The Defense* in *The New Republic* (1964), later anthologized in Updike's *Assorted Prose* (1965)

"And how could any writer survive such marrow-sucking reservations as these: Gilbert Highet worrying that 'he despises us, his readers'; the usually judicious Sir Herbert Read asserting that 'the talent (for genius is innocent) of a Vladimir Nabokov derives its energy from an obsessive hatred of the civilization it depicts'; and John Simon complaining 'nor do Nabokov's characters have that marvelous rightness of tone that, for example: C. P. Snow's have.' ... C. P. Snow!!"
    —Andrew Field in *TriQuarterly* (winter, 1970)

★ ★ ★ ★ ★ ★ ★ ★

"There are a few people in the Soviet Union who have actually managed to read almost all of Nabokov's prose works (even they are amazed to learn that Nabokov has written a substantial amount of poetry)—a feat that requires both luck and ingenuity. . . .

"The most interesting discussions of Nabokov currently focus on *Lolita,* and the things Russian readers catch sometimes escape American readers. For example, one well-known young poet who had read *Lolita* only in Russian pointed out a parody which few of Nabokov's American commentators have noticed—the poem Humbert reads to Quilty in the next to the last chapter ('Because you took advantage of a sinner') is a play on Eliot's 'Ash Wednesday.' Those who really like *Lolita* come alive when Nabokov's name is mentioned. One elderly scholar said she was astonished that such a subject could be both beautiful and tragic. A young translator enthusiastically read favorite passages (such as the execution of Quilty) and even quoted sections from memory. A professor of Russian literature... argued furiously with his wife—she attacked the 'what' of the novel and he defended the 'how.'

"Even Nabokov's most ardent fans dislike the Russian translation of *Lolita*. It is sad to report, but almost without exception Russians find Nabokov's translation clumsy and even ungrammatical; they express surprise that the author of *Dar* and *The Gift* and *Priglashenie na kaze (Invitation to a Beheading)* could write so poorly. (One linguist told me he found *Lolita* fascinating because it was written in a kind of dead language.) Of course, part of this is due to the fact that contemporary Soviet Russian is quite different from the Russian Nabokov once wrote, and there are many things he might not know (for example, that ordinary Russian for 'popcorn' is simply *popkorn*). But it was melancholy to hear a translator of poetry quote several lines of *Dar* from memory, then hold up the Russian *Lolita* and say, with a sigh, 'He has forgotten... he has forgotten.'

"On the other hand, virtually all Russians regard the prose of *Dar* and *Priglashenie na kazé* as unique in the history of Russian literature..."

—from "Nabokov's Russian Readers," by Ellendea Proffer, in *TriQuarterly* (winter, 1970)

"I am only troubled now by the jangling of my rusty Russian strings. The history of this translation is a history of disillusion. Alas, that 'marvelous Russian' which, I always thought, constantly awaited me somewhere, blooming like true spring behind hermetically sealed gates to which I kept the key for so many years—that Russian turns out to be non-existent. And behind the gates there is nothing, except charred stumps and a hopeless autumn vista; the key in my hand is more like a lock-pick."

—Nabokov's postscript (translated into English by Irwin Weil) to his Russian *Lolita*

★ ★ ★ ★ ★ ★ ★

"What is translation? On a platter
A poet's pale and glaring head,
A parrot's screech, a monkey's chatter,
And profanation of the dead.
The parasites you were so hard on

> *Are pardoned if I have your pardon,*
> *O, Pushkin, for my strategem:*
> *I traveled down your secret stem,*
> *And reached the root, and fed upon it;*
> *Then, in a language newly learned,*
> *I grew another stalk and turned*
> *Your stanza, patterned on a sonnet,*
> *Into my honest roadside prose—*
> *All thorn, but cousin to your rose."*
>
> —first stanza of poem "On Translating
> *Eugene Onegin"*(1955-67)

After the Bollingen Foundation, in 1964, issued Pushkin's *Onegin* in a four-volume translation with commentary by Nabokov, Robert Conquest wrote in the June, 1965, issue of *Poetry*: "It is sad to knock any attempt to bring Pushkin before us. There are long passages without these faults. Nevertheless, on the whole this is too much a transposition into Nabokovese, rather than a translation into English." And, in *The New York Review of Books* (July 15, 1965), Edmund Wilson (who had been very kind to Nabokov in his early days in America and had helped place *Bend Sinister* with a publisher) savaged his onetime protégé with a marathon critique that contended Nabokov "is torn between the culture he has left behind and that to which he is trying to adapt himself.... There is a drama in his *Evigeniy Onegin* which is not Onegin's drama. It is the drama of Nabokov himself trying to correlate his English and Russian sides." Wilson's attack—astonishing in its pedantry, pettiness, peevishness, and carelessness—even praises Sartre for his insights into Nabokov! It aroused (and deserved) a polemic masterpiece by Nabokov, "Reply to My Critics," published in *Encounter* (February, 1966) and anthologized in *Nabokov's Congeries* (Page Stegner, editor). The Wilson portion of Nabokov's reply began:

"The longest, most ambitious, most captious, and, alas, most reckless article is Mr. Edmund Wilson's . . . and this I now select for a special examination.

"A number of earnest simpletons consider Mr. Wilson to be an authority in my field ('he misses few of Nabokov's lapses,' as one hasty well-wisher puts it in a letter . . .), and no doubt such delusions should not be tolerated; still, I am not sure that the necessity to defend my work from blunt jabs and incompetent blame would have been a sufficient incentive for me to discuss that article, had I not been moved to do so by the unusual, unbelievable, and highly entertaining opportunity that I am unexpectedly given by Mr. Wilson himself of refuting practi-

cally every item of criticism in his enormous piece. The mistakes and misstatements in it form an uninterrupted series so complete as to seem artistic in reverse, making one wonder if, perhaps, it had not been woven that way on purpose to be turned into something pertinent and coherent when reflected in a looking glass. I am unaware of any other such instance in the history of literature. It is a polemicist's dream come true, and one must be a poor sportsman to disdain what it offers.

"As Mr. Wilson points out with such disarming good humor at the beginning of his piece, he and I are old friends. I fully reciprocate 'the warm affection sometimes chilled by exasperation' that he says he feels for me. When I first came to America a quarter of a century ago, he wrote to me, and called on me, and was most kind to me in various matters, not necessarily pertaining to his profession. I have always been grateful to him for the tact he showed in not reviewing any of my novels while constantly saying flattering things about me in the so-called literary circles where I seldom revolve. We have had many exhilarating talks, have exchanged many frank letters. A patient confidant of his long and hopeless infatuation with the Russian language and literature, I have invariably done my best to explain to him his monstrous mistakes of pronunciation, grammar, and interpretation. As late as 1957, at one of our last meetings, in Ithaca, upstate New York, where I lived at the time, we both realized with amused dismay that, despite my frequent comments on Russian prosody, he still could not scan Russian verse. Upon being challenged to read Evgeniy Onegin *aloud, he started to perform with great gusto, garbling every second word, and turning Pushkin's iambic line into a kind of spastic anapest with a lot of jaw-twisting haws and rather endearing little barks that utterly jumbled the rhythm and soon had us both in stitches.*

* * * * * * * *

POETRY READING AT THE "Y":

In her charming history of the Poetry Center at the Young Men's/Young Women's Hebrew Association (Y.M.-Y.W.H.A.) in Manhattan ("Ode to a 'Y' ," New York *Times Magazine*, March 31, 1974), Veronica Geng recalls the moment when "Vladimir Nabokov was solemnly introduced by Susan Sontag in terms like 'aesthetic bliss,' and then read a ballad about a peculiar family on a picnic, turning his elegant, measured voice and rolled r's to lines like:

"*Pauline had asthma, Paul used a crutch.*
They were cute little rascals but could not run much."

(The verse comes from a 1957 Nabokov poem, "The Ballad of Longwood Glen.")

★ ★ ★ ★ ★ ★ ★ ★

ON NABOKOV'S SEVENTIETH BIRTHDAY (1969):
"TO: V. Nabokov, Montreaux, Switzerland
"FROM: J. Barth, Buffalo, U.S.A.
"RE: April 23
"Dear Mr. N.:
"Today we lost Cervantes, St. George, and Shakespeare, but recouped Shakespeare and are clear ahead by Viscount Allenby, Admiral Anson, Hazel Brown, Sandra Dee, J.P. Donleavy, J. A. Froude, Raymond Huntley, Margaret Kennedy, Ngaio Marsh, Max Planck, I like Max Planck, Sergei Prokofiev, Henry Sherek, Vladimirs Sikorski and Yourself, Dame Ethel Smyth, Shirley Temple, and J. M. W. Turner. I guess we're OK. . . .

"He'll go far in time! My wish for him, before he outs that one brief candle: let today in 2899, when Earth sets about his Milennial *Festschrift,* Betelgeuse count a hundred on his cake!"

—John Barth, in *Triquarterly's* belated Festschrift (winter, 1970)

"Is seventy a 'human' age at which to have one's greatest book appear?

—Critic Richard Gilman, professor of drama at Yale

"At Cornell University, where he taught for a decade (1948-1958), Vladimir Nabokov would always begin his first lecture by saying, 'Great novels are above all great fairy tales. . . . Literature does not tell the truth but makes it up.' *Ada,* Nabokov's fifteenth novel, thirty-fifth book, and first new novel since *Pale Fire* (1962), is a great fairy tale, a supremely original work of the imagination. Published two weeks after Nabokov's seventieth birthday, it provides further evidence that he is a peer of Kafka, Proust, and Joyce, those earlier masters of totally unique universes of fiction.

"*Ada, or Ardor: A Family Chronicle* (its full title) is a love story, an erotic masterpiece, an Edenic fantasy, a philosophical investigation into the nature of time. Almost twice as long as any previous Nabokov novel, its rich and variegated prose moves from the darkest to the lightest of sonorities as Nabokov sensually evokes the widest range of delights."

—from Alfred Appel's front-page critique in the New York *Times Book Review,* May 4, 1969

AS *TIME* SEES *ADA*: "As an easy entry on the boy-meets-girl plot level, Nabokov indulges in a tale about Van Veen and his half sister Ada Veen. They fall in love at the respective ages of fourteen and twelve and begin an energetic sex life in the nooks and dells of the family's rural estate. Over the years, their floating orgy suffers prolonged periods of inactivity. In their old age, however, Van and Ada reunite and mate— now in a highly figurative way—melding into an unbeing that Nabokov calls Vaniada. Licensed allusion hunters will find that Vanadis is an epithet for Freya, the popular Swedish sex goddess who was also close to her brother.

"Nabokov sums up these amorous doings in a mock dust-jacket blurb that closes *Ada* by describing only the book's most superficial aspects. Long before he gets around to that, though, a suspicion has set in that the surface love story is as different from the real *Ada* as a bicycle reflector is from a faceted ruby. More even than *Lolita* and *Pale Fire*, *Ada* is studded with assaults and asides directed at literary forms, figures, and fashions. Along with its masquerade as a delicious *fin de siecle amour,* Nabokov provides the most unconventional commentary on the novel ever written.

"Beginning with an inversion of Tolstoy's remark that all happy families are alike, its early chapters plunge forward on rubble created by assaults on the mannerisms of regional romance and dynastic memoir. Science fiction, sexual symbolism, popular novels that get turned into movies come under fire. So do impressionistic translations. Characters mimic Jane Austen and Dickens. Poets Auden and Lowell are spliced into a modern entity called 'Lowden, a minor poet and translator.' The celebrated Argentine writer Jorge Luis Borges is yawned offstage as Osberg, a contriver of 'mystico-allegoric anecdotes.' Meanwhile, the children's flabby governess is writing Maupassant's *The Diamond Necklace* and Jean Cocteau's *Les Enfants Terribles,* an indication of Nabokov's opinion of both.

"To precis *Ada* as a love story is like describing *Lolita* as a cautionary tale for Girl Scouts. But the literary brickbats, too, as well as the snatches of Russian, the quadrilingual puns, the satiric undercuts, are all embellishments—provided partly to tease scholars, who are now so far behind Nabokov's accumulation of literary clues and *culs de sac* that it will take years of footnoting to catch up. (Ardis, the family seat, becomes Arrowhead Manor, *Le Château de la Fléche,* Fles Hall.)

"Nabokov's text, as often before, is disguised as an unpublished manuscript. It ostensibly reflects Van Veen's memories of his 83-

year-long affair with Ada. Yet, anyone who thinks that *Ada* is Van's book need only rearrange the letters of VAN'S BOOK until they spell NABOKOV'S. Once the creator's name has been uttered, *Ada's* profoundest purpose comes into view. *Lolita* displays more human feeling. But *Ada* is the supreme fictional embodiment of Nabokov's lifelong, bittersweet preoccupation with time and memory. Nabokov is acutely aware that it is only through memory that we possess the past. But how fragile that hold is—and how much art and individuality depend upon it!

"Tricks with time, thoughts on time, even a chapter on 'The Texture of Time' interweave *Ada*. The love story does not 'really' start until page 555, when a phone call from Ada to aging Van causes a chain reaction in his memory, linking the images of his youth and transforming the past into a 'glittering now.' Appearing late in the novel, the 'Texture' essay is a recondite attempt on Van's part to caress the essence of time with the same ardor with which he once possessed Ada.*

"It is futile. One can almost hear Van's creator sighing at these efforts to have carnal knowledge of the infinite. 'You lose your immortality when you lose your memory,' Van remarks at one point. 'And if you land on Terra Caelistis (Heaven), with your pillow and chamber pot, you are made to room not with Shakespeare or even Longfellow, but with guitarists and cretins.'

"*Ada* cannot rightfully be separated from its language, from the chaos of literary allusions, the geographical and genealogical data. But its glory rises from the fragrance of things that have been lost but cannot be forgotten. Central to its timelessness is the anachronistic world of Ada's and Van's youth. Known as Antiterra, it is physically like a mixture of pastoral 19th century Russia and Canada and the modern U.S.

"Antiterra's 'current events' roam timelessly between an imagined future, in which Mississippi is run entirely by Negroes, and a fabled past, in which the Criméan War, occurring in 1886, is fought with modern war planes. For a while, space and time are suspended. Ultra-modern 'dorophones' ring, planes fly, and magic carpets skim cool glades without so much as a patent pending.

"En route, some of the characters perish by fire, water, and air—fleeting reminders of a return to elemental states. Age comes fi-

---

*Like Quilty's death scene in *Lolita* and the poem *Pale Fire*, this crucial section seems to have been written at or near the outset of the novel's composition. *Ada's* initial working title was *The Texture of Time*, and in a National Educational Television interview filmed in 1965, Nabokov discusses what is now Part Four, though he makes it sound like the beginning of the book."—Alfred Appel, in TriQuarterly

nally. Time reasserts itself. As the artifice is revealed, one almost expects to hear the snap of Prospero's wand. For this is Nabokov's autumnal fairy tale. Though not his finest book, it is certainly his most brilliant attempt yet to ransack the images and thoughts of his own past and shape them into a glittering now of the imagination."—From *Time*'s cover story (cover line: "The Novel Is Alive and Living in Antiterra"; article title: "Prospero's Progress," May 23, 1969

"At a first reading *Ada* (in so many ways a variation on the themes of *Pale Fire*) seems to me self-indulgent and at many points irredeemably overwritten. The Newspeak of Ardor is often on the same predictable level of ingenuity as double-acrostics. The mixture of English, French, Russian, and private esperanto is labored. It is as if Nabokov had been mastered by that multilingual dilemma which has, until now, been so notably in his control. But with a writer of this reach, first readings are always inadequate. Lived with, the layer cake in *Ada* may prove a culinary find. It is, I feel, less profitable at this stage to debate over the merits or vices of 'Nabokese' than it is to throw light on its sources and fabrics."— George Steiner, Extraordinary Fellow of Churchill College, Cambridge, in *TriQuarterly* (winter, 1970)

"Chateaubriand and Byron are to *Ada* what Poe and Mériteé are to *Lolita*. Humbert continually calls Lolita 'Carmen,' and at tender and crucial moments quotes from Mériteé, a trap for the reader who concludes that Humbert will surely kill the deceitful enchantress, since Jose killed his Carmen. 'A damned good fool I have made of someone,' says the narrator of Nabokov's *Despair*."
—Alfred Appel in a *TriQuarterly* (winter, 1970) footnote

* * * * * * * *

"Did you hear that Gore Vidal has turned Catholic? he asks."
—from Israel Shenker's interview with Nabokov (New York *Times Book Review,* January 9, 1972)

Gore Vidal's reply (in a footnote to the same article): "It's the last thing in the world anybody could suggest about me. I would regard it as spontaneous total invention. Nabokov and I have a series of running jokes. We have a mutual friend, a lady, whom we send back and forth. The last time I sent her to Vlad, which is what I call him, I told her to tell him that I was putting him down for the Angela Davis Fund. He loathes my politics and I loathe his politics. I'm always trying to get him on the left and he's always trying to get me on the right."

★   ★   ★   ★   ★   ★   ★   ★

"*I would say that the main favor I ask of the serious critic is sufficient perceptiveness to understand that whatever term or trope I use, my purpose is not to be facetiously flashy or grotesquely obscure but to express what I feel and think with the utmost truthfulness and perception.*"—Interview with New York *Times* obituary writer Alden Whitman published on Nabokov's seventy-second birthday, April 23, 1971

TRANSPARENT THINGS:
"Nabokov's first new novel in three years yokes the themes of his early work to the style of the late—with singularly depressing results. He has always been a mannerist—elliptical, self-conscious, teasing and digressive—but his early fiction, first written in Russian, pleasingly conveyed romantic, ethereal stories through sensuous and unpretentious prose. His later work grew longer (Nabokov's most articulate supporters, Edmund Wilson and Mary McCarthy, collapsed before the onanistic concatenations of *Ada*). ... the effect is rather like a $2 Christmas tree hung with every baroque ornament that Nabokov could salvage from the Bolsheviks.... In *Ada,* an overpowering book, such pointless mannerisms could be overlooked: a trifle like *Transparent Things* crumbles beneath them."
—Review in *Newsweek,* November 20, 1972, by Peter S. Prescott, son of Orville Prescott, who wrote in the New York *Times,* August 18, 1958, that *Lolita* "is undeniably news in the world of books. Unfortunately, it is bad news. There are two equally serious reasons why it isn't worth any adult reader's attention. The first is that it is dull, dull, dull in a pretentious, florid and archly fatuous fashion. The second is that it is repulsive."

"History offered the gift of several lives to Vladimir Nabokov, and he made of it what we know: an odyssey of three languages, a stylish fable of émigrés and aristocrats which he conjured finally into English, and at least one masterpiece, *Lolita.* Since then, it is generally agreed, he has become America's foremost, one might say our official, literary stylist: prodigiously active, caustic; alternating brilliant new works with older ones from the emigre past, retooled into English either by himself or, usually, by his son Dmitri. ... If Nabokov's recent book *Transparent Things,* was a

farewell to literature, as some critics have guessed, then *A Russian Beauty* is a bit of tidying up."
—From review of *A Russian Beauty and Other Stories* in the New York *Times Book Review* (April 29, 1973), by Paul Zweig, chairman of Queens College's Department of Comparative Literature

"*I know nothing about butterflies, and indeed do not care for the fluffier night-flying ones, and would hate any of them to touch me: even the prettiest gives me a nasty shiver like some floating spider web or that bathroom pest on the Riviera, the silver louse.*"—Vadim Vadimovich, in Nabokov's 1974 novel, *Look at the Harlequins!*

"Who but Vladimir Nabokov would invent a fictional novelist for the sole purpose of comparing him unfavorably with Vladimir Nabokov? Vadim Vadimovich, the hero of *Look at the Harlequins!*, is a Russian émigré writer whose career 'slyly' parallels his creator's. They diverge significantly only in the quality of their works . . .

". . . While I suppose Mr. Nabokov is up to one of his metaphorical mirror tricks here, it seems to me that his sleight of hand has slipped up once again, leaving him in a cruelly exposed position. To say it plainly, the book strikes me as the production of an imagination paralyzed by vanity."—Anatole Broyard in the New York *Times*, October 10, 1974

"This is one of his better mirror-boxes, with the usual annoyances of the dictionary hunt ('photic,' 'fatidic') and teeth-grating jokes ('The car is not exactly a Royce, but it rolls,' or, worse, 'my Negro maid, little Nefertitty as I had dubbed her'). If you can put up with all this, the sensuality, elegance and sunny arrogance of the performance are disagreeably pleasant."
—*Newsweek* review by Walter Clemons of
Look at the Harlequins!

"For some years now, Vladimir Nabokov has been presenting the pleasant spectacle of a writer expanding at both ends—frontally, from the brow of the present, with each new novel in English, while one by one his Russian novels, in filial translations edited paternally, emerge from behind the hill of the past. In *Glory*, or *Podvig (The Exploit)*, as it once was, the final one of these, it is strange, and oddly warming, to find the experienced ironist in one of his first bouts with his own talent and its lifelong preoccupations. With emotions still limpidly trying on its first masks, memory with its jointures melting but still plain, and people still somewhat conventionally islanded in their own solitudes, not yet so clearly caught in the necromancer's palm . . .

"This is the young Nabokov's novel, but by the hazards of life and publication it can never be that for us. As with the young jacket-picture of the author at 34, with its gosling neck, high forehead and lips pursed in proud promise, we know what this book will be like when 'it' is old. When it will be rewritten by a stout, longer-nosed balletomane of butterflies, in the style of a prince with the irony to know he is a giraffe . . .

"We refrain . . . from comparing *Glory* to Tolstoy's *Childhood, Boyhood, and Youth,* having our own ideas on the whereabouts of Martin Edelweiss. Did he get back to Russia? Did he die? Death, as Nabokov has elsewhere suggested, is only a matter of style. Martin rests, with all his other future prototypes, in the brotherhood of language. A happy place, often especially for exiles. An eagle's eyrie, to which all may come." —Hortense Calisher reviewing *Glory* on the front page of the New York *Times Book Review,* January 9, 1972

* * * * * * * *

"They like to read to each other. They reread *War and Peace* in a motel in Montana a few years ago, and sad to say, Tolstoy flunked. 'He paled slightly' or 'Andrei half smiled,' quotes Vladimir condescendingly. 'Really.' Between Tostoy and Nabokov it is clear that Véra would choose Nabokov, and the dedication she brings to him is total. Recently Nabokov heard that John Crowe Ransom, whose poetry he greatly admires, was rewriting many of his old poems at the age of eighty and dismantling their classic beauty. Vladimir turned to Véra and said quietly, 'Never let me do that.' "
—From *Time* interview by Martha Duffy (May 23, 1969)

"My first duty after Sebastian's death was to go through his belongings. He had left everything to me and I had a letter from him instructing me to burn certain of his papers. It was so obscurely worded that at first I thought it might refer to rough drafts or discarded manuscripts, but I soon found out that, except for a few odd pages dispersed among other papers, he himself had destroyed them long ago, for he belonged to that rare type of writer who knows that nothing ought to remain except the perfect achievement: the printed book; that is actual existence is inconsistent with that of its spectre, the uncouth manuscript flaunting its imperfections like a revengeful ghost carrying its own head under its arm; and that for this reason the litter of the workshop, no matter its sentimental or commercial value, must never subsist."

From chapter 4 of *The Real Life of Sebastian Knight* (published 1941)

★ ★ ★ ★ ★ ★ ★ ★

"Advice to a Young Writer"

"If possible, be Russian. And live in another country. Play chess. Be an active trader between languages. Carry precious metals from one to the other. Remind us of Stravinsky. Know the names of plants and flying creatures. Hunt gauzy wings with snares of gauze. Make science pay tribute. Have a butterfly known by your name.

"Do not be awed by giant predecessors. Be ill-tempered with their renown. Point out flaws. Frighten interviewers from *Time*. Appear in *Playboy*. Sell to the movies.

"Use unlikely materials. Who would choose Pnin as a hero, but how did we live before Pnin?

"Delight in peversity. Put a noun into the dictionary. Now we recognize the Lolita at every street corner, see her sucking sweetened milk through straws at every soda fountain, dream her through all our fantasies.

"Burn pedants in pale fire. Accept no fashions. Be your own fashion. Do not rely on earlier triumphs. Be new at each appearance.

"Age indomitably, in the European manner. Do not finish your labors young. Be a planet, not a meteor. Honor the working day. Sit at your desk.

"Not all of this is possible for you. But it is possible for Vladimir N., perched on his hill in Switzerland."

—Irwin Shaw in *TriQuarterly* (winter, 1970)

3
EXPERIENCING VLADIMIR NABOKOV

Lolita, light of my library, gem of literature. You "may well be the funniest tragedy since [Euripides wrote] *Hecuba*" (Howard Nemerov in *Kenyon Review*) and you are "the funniest book I remember having read" (John Hollander in *Partisan Review*). You have been made in the movies (by Stanley Kubrick, no less), denounced in the House of Commons, banned in England and France, Burma and Belgium, Austria and Australia. To some bookwatchers, you were "the filthiest book I've ever read," "exquisitely distilled sewage," "corrupt," "repulsive," "dirty," "decadent," "disgusting," and "dull, dull, dull." To Jack Kerouac, you were nothing more than a classic old bag of a love story, that's all.

Lo-lee-ta. I have adored you, pockmarked with typos, in the slime-green plain wrapping with which the Parisian pornographer Maurice Girodias decked you for your first outing (Olympia Press, 1955). I have devoured you repeatedly in your American hardcover (Putnam, 1958), on whose white jacket the misspelled critic Richard "Schikel" (no relation to your grieving Dick Schiller, Oh-my-out-of-earshot-goodbye Dolly!) praised you as "the most remarkable—and certainly the most original—novel written in English." I have ravaged you and you have ravished me in many paperbacks and I have stood by helplessly (and even enjoying) watching you being dissected in Alfred Appel's *Annotated Lolita* (McGraw-Hill). I have heard how, when you were very young, one publisher's reader saw Humbert Humbert and you as "Old Europe debauching young America" while another saw "Young America debauching old Europe"; both rejected you. No matter, no matter now, for the joke is on them and all of us. And, as our century enters its final years, the last laugh may yet be the best of all: *The Great American Novel was written by a Russian.*

The magnitude of the achievement is overwhelming. The comparison most often made is to the sailor born Teodor Jozef Konrad Korzeniowski in Poland in 1857 who died in England in 1924 as the writer Joseph Conrad. But Conrad was a literary novice of thirty when he started to write English, while Nabokov was a middle-aged refugee with nine novels and nine plays behind him in his native Russian. And no sooner had *Lolita* poked her head above the counter in American bookstores in 1958 than another Conrad—Conrad Brenner—wrote a prophetic critique in *The New Republic:*

> Vladimir Nabokov is an artist of the first

rank, a writer in the great tradition. He will never win the Pulitzer Prize or the Nobel Prize, yet *Lolita* is probably the best fiction to come out of this country (so to speak) since Faulkner's burst in the thirties. He may be the most important writer now going in this country. He is already, God help him, a classic. He has written in Russian, French, German, and now wields an English that a native young writer would kill for. I am afraid that, in this respect, he puts Conrad in the shade. Where Conrad creaks, Nabokov dances.

And, lest *Lolita* look like a one-time wonder, Mary McCarthy hailed Nabokov's next published novel, *Pale Fire* (1962), as "a creation of perfect beauty, symmetry, strangeness, originality, and moral truth. Pretending to be a curio, it cannot disguise the fact that it is one of the very great works of art of this century, the modern novel that everyone thought was dead and that was only playing possum."

Let John Updike play with himself over whether Nabokov is "now an American writer and the best living" (*TriQuarterly*, 1970) or "the best writer of English prose at present holding American citizenship" (*New Republic*, 1964). *You* should float like a butterfly above all this nitpicking on Nabokov's stature. You should discover, or rediscover, his *Lolita* right away. Read her for pleasure. Have your hedonistic way with her. Don't study her; don't analyze her—not the first time, anyway. Enjoy her. Enjoy her.

The first time I picked her up—as a GI in Paris—I thought I was buying a piece of porn. And, indeed, *Lolita* is the most satisfying—perhaps the *only* satisfying—work of erotic literature I have have yet to read. But, by the time Humbert Humbert had his way with Lolita thrice in one morning a third of the way through *Lolita*, I knew that he and I were pursuing an obsession to an inevitable end that neither he could fathom nor I could guess.

I read on—and, as he and she (and I) set sail through a Motel America I recognized, but had never seen this way, with "instructions posted above the toilet (on whose tank the towels were unhygienically heaped) asking guests not to throw into its bowl garbage, beer cans, cartons, stillborn babies" ... up-and-down highways glittering with neon-glowing Greek mythology: Humbert refuels "under the sign of Pegasus" (Mobilgas) while

Lolita sneaks a leak and a phone call at "the sign of the Conche" (Shell) . . . sharing his disappointment (and her unawareness and my own realization) that the Appalachia which had loomed large in his imagination "as a gigantic Switzerland or even Tibet, all mountain, glorious diamond peak upon peak, giant conifers . . . and Red Indians under the catalpas . . . all boiled down to a measly surburban lawn and a smoking garbage incinerator."

It was a revelation, this America which Nabokov invented and we already lived in: progressive girls' camps, where little lolitas made X-ray pictures, called shadowgraphs, of each other's bones for "educational" recreation ./. . the art around us: "conventionally primitive eyes, sliced guitars, blue nipples and geometrical designs of the day" . . . fan magazines and funnies:

> . . . A handsome, very ripe actress with huge lashes and a pulpy red underlip, endorsing a shampoo. Ads and fads. Young scholars dote on plenty of pleats. . . . It is your hostess' duty to provide robes. Unattached details take all the sparkle out of your conversation. All of us have known "pickers"—one who picks her cuticle at the office party. Unless he is very elderly or very important, a man should remove his gloves before shaking hands with a woman. Invite Romance by wearing the Exciting New Tummy Flattener. Trims tums, nips hips. Tristram in Movielove. Yessir! The Joe-Roe marital enigma is making yaps flaps. Glamourize yourself quickly and inexpensively. Comics. Bad girl dark hair fat father cigar; good girl red handsome daddums clipped mustache . . .

Movies: Lolita favored backstage musicals and what Humbert calls "westerners" and "underworlders" in which "telephone bills ran to billions" . . . and an uncanny émigré ear to how we sounded early into the Helen Gurley Brown Era: "Maffy On Say," says Bill Mead introducing his fiance . . . "one was bound to have a few amiable fine-dayers yelping at you" . . . or the sound of a three-folding phone booth door: "Ah-ah-ah."

When *Lolita* was over, I was thrilled—and I waited only a month to try her again: the outcome no longer in doubt, but reveling in Humbert's infinite variations, both poetic and clinical, on nymphets and his own nympholepsy . . . the many clues that Clare Quilty planted before his abduction . . . Humbert's and Lolita's first quarrel: "At the hotel we had separate rooms, but in the middle of the night she came sobbing into mine, and we made it up very gently. You see, she had absolutely nowhere else to go" . . . the great love poem ("Wanted, wanted: Dolores Haze") and the whining country-musical death poem parodizing Eliot in passing ("Because you took advantage of a sinner") that follows Humbert's epic death tussle with Quilty (stylized violence: "I felt suffocated as he rolled over me. I rolled over him. We rolled over me. They rolled over him. We rolled over us") . . . and just the verbal imagination that names a White Russian cab driver Taxovich or calls one's tragic destiny McFate.

Not all my GI buddies and other friends back home enjoyed *Lolita* a much as I did. The common complaint was that "I lost interest in (or couldn't finish) the second half"—which is where Humbert's sexual quest, having climaxed, wanes, and Nabokov's American landscape asserts itself. (Nabokov confesses to seeing himself not as a landscape artist, but as a landless escape artist.) Although *Lolita* stayed atop the best-seller list for a year, largely because of her notoriety, librarians reported that many borrowers brought her back unfinished. In his introduction to *The Annotated Lolita,* Alfred Appel tells how his fellow GI, "Stockade Clyde" Carr, said "Hey, lemme read your dirty book, man!," skipped the foreword, read through the first paragraph, and then flung the fragile Olympia Press edition against the wall, exclaiming: "Damn! It's God-damn Litachure!" Appel writes that less perceptive "critics and remedial readers who complain that the second half of *Lolita* is less interesting are not aware of the possible significance of their admission." And the advice here is *not* to read *Lolita* as a dirty book, but to enjoy her dirty tricks (and all her other magical pranks) as they happen to you.

Pnin (published 1957) was written *after Lolita* and *before Pale Fire,* but, thanks again to *Lolita*'s international notoriety, *Pnin* was published in America *before Lolita.* Thus, poor *Pnin* is often misunderstood as pre-*Lolita* Nabokov. The Victorian gentility of *Pnin*'s prose tends to enhance the illusion. (Would Humbert Humbert ever refer to a "bright pat of dog dirt somebody had already slipped upon"? And would the Nabokov of *Lolita* let it slip by unembroidered?) But it is wisest to read Nabokov's three best American novels in sequence: *Lolita* then *Pnin,* then *Pale Fire.* For, in between two masterpieces (and the air of the latter will be much more rarefied than the first's), *Pnin* dwells as a breather or a plateau—not down-to-earth, but sufficiently high, very sunny, and somewhat revealing.

Not that Timofey Pavlovich Pnin—who orders "viscous-and-sawdust" when he wants whisky-and-soda, and who Pninizes a series of boarding-house rooms with a coffee grinder "which was not quite as good as the one that had exploded last year" and "a couple of alarm clocks running the same race every night"—is Vladimir Vladimirovich Nabokov, who knew English better than Russian in his boyhood and who went the Cambridge-Berlin émigré route while Pnin took the Prague-Paris trail after fleeing Leninized Russia. In fact, Nabokov is the narrator of *Pnin*, as he hints by a semigratuitous "with my help" planted early in chapter 1. Several other clues are planted before a butterfly interlude in chapter 5 elicits the comment "Pity Vladimir Vladimirovich is not here" from Pnin's friend Chateau; "I have always had the impression that his entomology was merely a pose," Pnin responds. There is also a reference to the emigre writer Sirin (Nabokov's pseudonym for his Russian novels). Then, in chapter 7, narrator Vladimir Vladimirovich steps onstage. He is a past lover of the atrocious woman who made Pnin her past husband. He is part of the human wedge that will dislodge Pnin from a potentially secure future with tenure at Waindell College.

No, Nabokov is not Pnin and Pnin is not Nabokov. But *Pnin* expresses a Nabokov between two worlds: the coeval Pnins that he was outdistancing and the America so lovingly embraced by an outsider in *Lolita*. But is it Nabokov or Pnin who immortalizes the sound of an American pencil sharpener ("that goes ticonderoga-ticonderoga, feeding on the yellow finish and sweet wood and ends up in a kind of soundlessly spinning ethereal void as we all must")? Who regrets that Shakespeare-in-English doesn't sound as good as in the Russian originals of his youth? Who teaches Russian to a girl who wants to read *Anna Karamazov* in the original and to a linguist named McBeth "whose prodigious memory had already disposed of ten languages and was prepared to entomb ten more" under the auspices of a college president who pays homage to "Russia—the country of Tolstoy, Stanislavski, Raskolnikov, and other great and good men"? Which man, Nabokov or Pnin, dissolves in tears of homesickness at a shamelessly banal Soviet documentary film? Which lover is more offended by the post-Freudian therapist who even calls Siamese twins "a group" and makes off with Pnin's wife, Liza? Or by the chairman of French Literature and Language who dislikes literature and has no French, but travels "tremendous distances to attend Modern Language conventions at which he would flaunt his ineptitude as if it were some majestic whim, and parry with great thrusts of healthy lodge humor any attempt to inveigle him into the subtleties of the parley-voo"?

We can wonder, but we need not probe. Just relax and enjoy and laugh a little. *Pnin* is first-rate Nabokov written in the autumnal mood of a northern campus in November and marred only by the episodic form that may have been right for *The New Yorker* (where chapters 1, 3, 4, and 6 originally appeared, according to my Avon paperback edition), but leaves the reader a little more tantalized than satisfied. Or, as Pnin might put it: "A genius needs to keep so much in store and thus cannot offer you the whole of himself as I do."

Everything is before your eyes in *Pale Fire* (1962)—but what a great trick the old magician has pulled off with nothing but sheer genius up his sleeve!

At first, *Pale Fire* appears to parodize *The Annotated Lolita* (1970), which was yet to come. After a brief quote from Boswell, it offers a scholarly yet provocative foreword by an editor-annotator named Dr. Charles Kinbote, with only a few minor digressions. ("There is a vary loud amusement park right in front of my present lodgings.") Kinbote tells us that we are about to read a 999-line poem by an Appalachian college poet named John Francis Shade (1898-1959) and that it will be followed by Kinbote's notes:

> Although those notes, in conformity with custom, come after the poem, the reader is advised to consult them first and then study the poem with their help, rereading them of course as he goes through its text, and perhaps, after having done with the poem, consulting them a third time so as to complete the picture. I find it wise in such cases as this to eliminate the bother of back-and-forth leafings by either cutting out and clipping together the pages with the text of the thing, or, even more simply, purchasing two copies of the same work which can then be placed in adjacent positions on a comfortable table—not like the shaky little affair on which my typewriter is precariously enthroned now, in

> this wretched motor lodge, with that carrousel inside and outside my head,

—which seems a wizard's clever ploy to make sales double, but is not necessarily the only or best way to read *Pale Fire*.

The poem, "Pale Fire," follows—and it is a semi-polished, unsurpassably easy-to-read mediocrity. It comes in four cantos, bearing no resemblance, living or dead, to those of Ezra Pound, but a great likeness to imitation Robert-Frost-at-his-most-mediocre; in fact, Shade boasts (in lines 424-426) that his name was twice bandied *"just behind (one oozy footstep) Frost."* There is also a dry, faculty-lounge armchair tone of a withered heterosexual aping the aging W. H. Auden. Canto 1 is formal wordplay mixed with autobiography, intonations of mortality, and little academic graffiti like "RED SOX BEAT YANKS 5-4 ON CHAPMAN'S HOMER" dutifully explained by Kinbote. Canto 2, twice as long, tells, among other things, of the death of Shade's ungainly daughter: so backward a girl, in fact, that the word "pot" came out "top;" "spider," "redips;" "powder," "red wop"; and, in Kinbote's note, "T. S. Eliot," "toilest." (Auden, on the other hand, preferred the anagram "toilets" for "T. S. Eliot.") Canto 3, just as long as canto 2, resumes the themes of canto 1 and has Shade confront a vision of the afterlife marred by a typographical error. Canto 4 promises everything:

> Now I shall spy on beauty as none has
> Spied on it yet. Now I shall cry out as
> None has cried out. Now I shall try what none
> Has tried. Now I shall do what none has done.

and, eighty-six trivial lines later, *"Now I shall speak of evil as none has Spoken before . . ."** But what does Shade deliver? Naught but the soggy metaphor of the poet shaving in his bathtub and a long list of petty dislikes. Even poor Kinbote has to admit that

> The poet like a fiery rooster seems to flap his wings in a preparatory burst of would-be inspiration, but the sun does not rise. Instead of the wild poetry promised here, we get a jest or two, a bit of satire, and at the end of the canto, a wonderful radiance of tenderness and repose.

minutes before, as Kinbote has already hinted, Shade met his tragic end.

---

*See Part 2 above for quotation from this Section.

The poem over, we are not quite a quarter of the way into the slender volume, *Pale Fire*. We are scarcely prepared, however, for what awaits us in Kinbote's "Commentary," which is the body of the book. Suddenly, we are plunged into a Graustarkian fairy tale—or is it madness? Or metrics? Or, perchance, reality?—of the lost kingdom of Zembla. Charles Kinbote, we perceive, is the lost monarch of that faraway land: a fugitive king, the homosexual Charles the Beloved, fleeing the Bolsheviks who have collectivized his throne and are hunting him down even in the grove of Academe. John Shade, we realize, will die of an assassin's bullet meant for Kinbote. We read on, enthralled by Charles the Beloved's escape from Zembla, his marriage-of-inconvenience with his exiled queen Disa, and how Nabokov is working out the ultimate confrontation of Shade and Kinbote with their destiny in the form of Jakob Gradus (1915-1959), alias Jack Degree, de Grey, d'Argus, Vinogradus, Leningradus, and Gray.

Perhaps the least appetizing villain Nabokov has ever put before us—"a Jack of small trades and a killer"—Gradus gives greatness to *Pale Fire* and the inspired form Nabokov has imposed upon the novel. Unlike earlier *(The Real Life of Sebastian Knight)* and later *(Ada)* variations, *Pale Fire* is the one with the *Seven Days to Noon* movie momentum which tells us that, even while we are reading about the poet and the king of Zembla, a murderer is hurtling toward them and us. For the plodding Gradus is a speeding metaphor, too, as Nabokov notes in Kinbote's notes:

> The force propelling him is the magic action of Shade's poem itself, the very mechanism and sweep of verse, the powerful iambic motor. Never before has the inexorable advance of fate received such a sensuous form (for other images of that transcendental tramp's approach see note to line 17),

where, much earlier, Nabokov had promised:

> We shall accompany Gradus in constant thought, as he makes his way from distant dim Zembla to green Appalachia, through the entire length of the poem, following the road of its rhythm, riding past in a rhyme, skidding around the corner of a run-on, breathing with the caesura, swinging down to the foot of the page from line to line as from

branch to branch, hiding between two words (see note to line 596), reappearing on the horizon of a new canto, steadily marching nearer in iambic motion, crossing streets, moving up with his valise on the escalator of the pentameter, stepping off, boarding a new train of thought, entering the hall of a hotel, putting out the bedlight, while Shade blots out a word and falling asleep as the poet lays down his pen for the night.

One hideous joke of all this is that Kinbote had moved next door to Shade in the hope that his friendly reminiscences would inspire Shade to reassemble Zembla in verse—and this is what he expected the poem "Pale Fire" to do. In the bloody climax of mistaken identity—that brief minute when Shade and Kinbote and Gradus are alive and together for the first and last time—Kinbote took possession of the manuscript. That night, he discovered, to his horror, that the poem had next-to-naught to do with Zembla: the poet had obliterated the land Charles the Beloved loved almost as effectively as the usurpers had. But, no matter! He would read meanings into and out of Shade's poem—and who will ever dare say that what he has done is unprecedented in Academia?

If *Pale Fire* is a masterpiece of pedantry as well as literature, it will nevertheless delight you. For every difficulty along the route, there is a Nabokovian delight. We meet old friends: the head of the Russian department at Wordsmith College (where Kinbote rents the home of a Judge Goldsworth)* is Professor Pnin ("a farcical pedant of whom the less said the better") and Shade's poem offers this weather report:

> It was a year of Tempests; Hurricane
> Lolita swept from Florida to Maine.

If that isn't enough, Kinbote's note to line 413, which begins "*A nymph came pirouetting . . .* " informs us that, in Shade's earlier draft, there was "the lighter and more musical: *A nymphet pirouetted.*" Other incidental delights include a definition of certain

---

*Though I had gathered Kinbote might be a madman, not a king, and Gradus a creation of *his* imagination, the Princeton Slavonicist Nina Berberova's interpretation eluded me in two readings of *Pale Fire*, but checked out on third reading: "Some time ago, Judge Goldsworth had put an assassin in a lunatic asylum; this man had recently escaped and was searching for the judge to avenge himself. On one summer evening Kinbote and Shade were walking between their houses. The killer appeared, mistook Shade in the darkness for the judge (they were slightly alike) and shot him." (TriQuarterly, winter, 1970)

kinds of footnotes as "the rogue's galleries of words," Nabokov's use *(Bozhe moy!)* of the *Time* word "cinemactress," and this wonderful misadventure in translation of a letter from Queen Disa in Nice to King Charles the Beloved under royal house-arrest in the Zemblan capital of Ohnava:

> When the Zemblan Revolution broke out (May 1, 1958), she wrote the King a wild letter in governess English, urging him to come and stay with her until the situation cleared up. The letter was intercepted by the Ohnava police, translated into crude Zemblan by a Hindu member of the Extremist party, and then read aloud to the royal captive in a would-be ironic voice by the preposterous commandant of the palace. There happened to be in that letter one—only one, thank God—sentimental sentence: "I want you to know that no matter how much you hurt me, you cannot hurt my love," and this sentence (if we re-English it from the Zemblan) came out as: "I desire you and love when you flog me."

The last part of *Pale Fire* is a brief, prankish index—useful for reference while reading Kinbote's "Commentary" and a playful entity in itself. If you want to be gently victimized, look up "Andronikov" and "Niagarin" and follow directions. If you wonder what Shade's pastime of Word Golf was, look it up in the index and soon you'll be playing it: going from *love* to *hate* in three moves, *dead* to *live* in five.

When *Pale Fire* first appeared, Robert Martin Adams in the *Hudson Review* proclaimed Nabokov a "fish perpetually and magnificently out of water; long may he wave." Adams also wondered:

> Who, save this rococo gambler, would try to tell the story of an international political assassination in a set of lunatic footnotes to an atrocious poem in monstrous heroic couplets? Who else could be convulsively funny in an index? Trickery on this outrageous scale is, fortunately, rare in the novel; otherwise our responses would be debauched in half a season. But the master at the top of his form is an experience not to be missed . . .

I have found it most practical to experience *Pale Fire* by reading it straight through, but keeping a bookmark up front in Shade's poem for frequent referring-back rather than doing any referring-forward (except to the index). But perhaps the best advice of all is Nabokov's—or, rather, Shade's—on teaching Shakespeare at college level, quoted in Kinbote's note to line 172:

"First of all, dismiss ideas, and social background, and train the freshman to shiver, to get drunk on the poetry of *Hamlet* or *Lear*, to read with his spine and not with his skull."

These words are well appropriated — for *Lolita* and *Pale Fire* are Nabokov's *Hamlet* and *Lear*. Even *Pale Fire*'s title comes from Shakespeare, though you won't find its source in its pages. The source is act 4, scene 3 of *Timon of Athens:*

> The sun's a thief, and with his great attraction
> Robs the vast sea: the moon's an arrant thief
> And her pale fire she snatches from the sun:
> The sea's a thief, whose liquid surge resolves
> The moon into salt tears: the earth's a thief
> That feeds and breeds by a composture stolen
> From general excrement: each thing's a thief.

Such is Nabokov's dissembling in *Pale Fire*, though, that Kinbote is using the authorized Zemblan translation of *Timon* by his uncle Conmal, duke of Aros (1855-1955) and re-Englishing it back at us (in his note to Shade's lines 39-40) as:

> The sun is a thief: she lures the sea
> and robs it. The moon is a thief:
> he steals his silvery light from the sun.
> The sea is a thief: it dissolves the moon.

... and Shakespeare and Shade's and Nabokov's title. Later, in his note to line 962 *(". . . Help me, Will!* Pale Fire"), Nabokov-Kinbote gleefully misleads us thusly: "Paraphrased, this evidently means: let me look in Shakespeare for something I might use for a title. And the find is 'pale fire.' But in which of the Bard's works did our poet cull it? My readers must make their own research. All I have with me is a tiny vest pocket edition of *Timon of Athens*—in Zemblan! It certainly contains nothing that could be regarded as an equivalent of 'pale fire' . . ." Alas, poor Kinbote.

Try to imagine reading Chekhov or Tolstoy in a tongue that is native to him and you, instead of in translation, and you may begin to contemplate the next-best thing: the adventure that lies ahead.

Nabokov, having mastered and enriched the English language, took his nine Russian novels of the twenties and thirties and not only translated them (usually in collaboration) throughout the sixties, but rewrote them in the style of the mature wizard—not, fortunately, the tired wordsmith of the post-*Ada* seventies. Nabokov's Englishings were not published in the same order as their Russian originals, so today's reader is more fortunate than the critics who reviewed them out of sequence. The critics can pretend to have omniscience, but we, in fact, possess a semblance of it—and that possibility only since late 1971, when the series was completed. Nowadays, we can read Nabokov's nine from his past in the order in which they were written—observing and marveling at the growth of the writer; stumbling a little when he stumbles (usually from ambition rather than carelessness); and smiling to ourselves when we perceive the germ of a Lolita here and a Humbert there.

Published next to last in the series, *Mary* (1970), alias *Mashenka* (1926), deserves immediate attention not only because it is Nabokov's first novel, but because it just happens to be a good novel. (The translation is by Michael Glenny in collaboration with the author.) In his 1970 introduction, Nabokov admits to "no embarrassment in confessing to the sentimental stab of my attachment to my first book. Its flaws, the artifacts of innocence and inexperience, which any criticule could tabulate with jocose ease," are intact because he realized from the outset of his collaboration with Glenny that "our translation should be as faithful to the text as I would have insisted on its being had that text not been mine." So we are given, for once, an opaque glimpse of how the master wrote as a novice without the usual retouching job four decades later.

Don't be put off by its opening scene. It reads like Solzhenitsyn's *First Circle* and every other old-fangled Russian novel you may have read. Trapped in the dark of a *kaput* elevator in a Berlin *pension* in 1923, Aleksey Ivanovich Alfyorov introduces himself to "Lev Glevo. Lev Glebovich?" and the other party, identified two lines later as Ganin (and later as Lyovuska and Lyova), says "yes, it is." These two Russian emigres have never met before and are soon freed from the lift, but their lives are inextricably bound together by Mary, who "had first surrendered her profound, unique fragrance" to Ganin back in pre-revolutionary Russia, but later married Alfyorov, a vulgar little man with yellow, twitching beard. And Mary is at long last coming out of Russia on Saturday to rejoin Alfyorov, but, when Ganin learns who Alfyorov's wife is, he plans and plots (and expects) her running off with her first lover, himself, Lev Glevo, Lev Glebovich, Lyovushka, Lyova, Ganin, all of him.

From the moment of realization and the beginning of expectation, *Mary* moves forward cinematically and irresistibly toward the moment of Mary's arrival at 8:05 A.M. Saturday. Nabokov's first novel travels smoothly through the texture of time on two levels: forward in framework through the six days of awaiting Mary; and forward in flashback as Ganin relives their romance a little at a time, savoring and cherishing each phase, so that memory and reality will fuse, not collide, at the station on Saturday. But, because memory has always meant more to Nabokov than reality, there is a surprise ending on the last of his 114 pages. You will forgive me (and I trust Nabokov will) if I don't divulge it. But I think you will agree with me that it is the only good kind of surprise in literature: an inevitable, logical, justifiable one.

Ganin has a girlfriend—with whom he has wanted to break off almost from the moment he first possessed her on the floor of a moving taxi. The imminence of Mary's arrival hastens the breakup—but not before a splendidly cinematic scene in a cinema, where Ganin sits between his girl friend and *her* girl friend, who harbors a secret passion for Ganin and lives in the same boarding house. Ganin—who has worked in Berlin as a waiter, a movie extra, a salesman, and a compositor in a printing plant—finds the film thrilling, but the girls chat across him. Suddenly, he sees himself on the screen while the girls talk on, ignoring both the real him and his screen image. Later, Ganin walks home, thinking about how his shadow will wander from city to city, screen to screen, and he will never know who is seeing it and where it is roaming.

This scene is significant, in addition to being beautifully done. It introduces the *Doppelgänger* motif that repeats itself throughout Nabokov's work. (Humbert and Quilty are reverse doubles and Humbert Humbert's double name is significant. Even the unique Pnin has a double on another campus, who may somehow be Nabokov. And you probably haven't read *Despair* or *The Eye* yet.) The screen scene also epitomizes the mood of *Mary*. It is Ganin's shadow that lodges in the pre-*Cabaret*, pre-Isherwood Berlin boarding house and wanders through a two-dimensional Berlin of double-decker buses, smoky beer halls, and asphalt squares "while he himself was in Russia, reliving his memories as though they were reality."

> By the second week of August in northern Russia there is already a touch of autumn in the air. Every now and again a small yellow leaf falls from a birch tree; the broad fields, already harvested, have a bright autumnal emptiness. Along the forest's edge, where an expanse of tall grass spared by the haymakers shows its sheen to the wind, torpid bumblebees sleep on the mauve cushions of scabious flowers. And one afternoon, in a pavilion of the park—

Throughout *Mary*, a remembered landscape of a bygone Russia is re-created far more vividly than the Berlin in which the novel was set and written. As a dying poet remarks in the pages of *Mary*: "We should love Russia. Without the love of us emigres, Russia is finished. None of the people there love her."

Thus, nearly half a century ago, Nabokov was articulating his own tragedy and his uniqueness while flourishing a few of his other trademarks: wooing with words ("Macaroni grows in Italy," he tells Mary. "When still small it's called vermicelli. That means Mike's worms in Italian"). And fluttering by with a butterfly at a crucial moment ("There was something touching and wonderful about the way their letters managed to pass across the terrible Russia of that time—like a cabbage white butterfly flying over the trenches").

When he conceived his second novel, *King Queen Knave,* in the summer of 1927, Nabokov found that the "happy humidity" of *Mary* "was all very well but the book no longer pleased me (as it pleases me now for new reasons). The émigré characters I had collected in that display box were so transparent to the eye of the era that one could easily make out the labels behind them. . . . I felt no inclination to persevere in a technique assignable to the French 'human document' type, with a hermetic community faithfully described by one of its members. . . ."

By the time *King Queen Knave* was finished a year later, Nabokov had been living in Berlin for half a dozen years, but spoke no German, had no German friends, and had not read a single German novel, not even in translation. Yet, unlike most of his other Russian novels, this one is set largely in Berlin and entirely within German borders. Its people are German, though Nabokov admits that "I might have staged *KQKn* in Rumania or Holland. Familiarity with the map and weather of Berlin settled my choice."

Nearly forty years later, Nabokov could write, "Of all my novels, this bright brute is the gayest"—and, while one might champion long segments of *Pnin* and even *Lolita* for that honor, I would rank *KQKn* among the best second novels I've ever read. But I would caution you against making up such a list, for *KQKn* in its present (and undoubtedly best) form might not qualify. Carl R. Proffer, then of Indiana University, read the original 1928 edition in Russian and wrote about the changes Nabokov wrought in the 1968 English version. Just one small part of Professor Proffer's essay on "A New Deck for Nabokov's Knaves" (*TriQuarterly*, winter, 1970) is covered in the following passages:

> A pungent and gory category of additions to *KQKn* is formed by what can be called, hesitantly, "dirty details." The English version of the novel is more frankly and grotesquely ribald than its Russian draft. While it is true that death and murder are important themes, it sometimes seems that scatology precedes eschatology. Nabokov has interpolated so many toilets that the novel could be called "Royal Flush" as well as "Bright Brute."

Proffer goes on, citing page references, to show that Nabokov has also mixed in explicit references to homosexuality, simultaneous incest, masturbation, menstruation, prophylactics, a douche bag handed down from generation to generation, and hints of necrophilia. "The profusion of new private parts," says Proffer, "calls to mind a madman merrily decorating a Christmas tree . . . with male genitalia. . . . In non-sexual subdivisions of this category, one might put the new enthusiastic allusions to mucus . . . the incinerated monkey, and Martha's amusing amputee."

Proffer points out that, in all of these descriptions, "Nabokov's gusto instills disgust . . . which, along with humor, is presumably his goal." And, if Nabokov had a good time doing it to himself, we should have at least as good a time reading the result. We can rejoice that details he deems essential are now tolerated. But, if some cultural used-car salesman or other should try to tell you that the 1928-model Nabokov purrs along with the fluid drive of today's most avant-garde videos or slickest TV commercial (two intertwined arts), you ought to know that it's been reupholstered, particularly its back seat.

The King of *KQKn* is Kurt Dreyer, fifty, a merchant prince (and practical joker, though identities are seldom blurred in early Nabokov) and perhaps the healthiest trophy in the display case of human monsters with whom the old butterfly hunter has peopled his pages for half a century. Dreyer is the kind of man who takes his perspiring companions walking on the sunny side of the street on a hot day because, if he enjoys the sun, so will they. Alive and atingle, with all his antennae out, Dreyer finds interest and irony and laughter in the most pitiful individual or uneventful auto accident, but all his observations and judgments are superficialities-indepth. "The bright perception became the habitual abstraction," Nabokov writes of Dreyer. "Natures like his spend enough energy in tackling with all the weapons and vessels of his mind the enforced impressions of existence to be grateful for the neutral film of familiarity that soon forms between the newness and the consumer. It was too boring to think that the object might change of its own accord and assume unforseen characteristics. That would mean having to enjoy it again, and he was no longer young." And so he remains oblivious to the crumbling fidelity of this *Frau*.

The Queen of *KQKn* is Dreyer's wife, Martha, thirty-four, whose vibrant petulance and narrow bitchery are scathingly limned by the new *and* the old Nabokov in page after passionate page that make one care and even grieve for what becomes of this toadlike female. Though her husband has enough spare cash to circle the globe many times, Martha "would refuse to come, preferring a trim surburban lawn to the most luxuriant jungle." While Nabokov, in his 1967 preface to his own and his son's translation, disavows any knowledge of Balzac and Dreiser and "their preposterous stuff," he does confess to familiarity with *Madame Bovary* and *Anna Karenina,* as is obvious when, nearly halfway through *KQKn,* he says of Martha: "She was no Emma and no Anna. In the course of her conjugal life, she had grown accustomed to grant her favors to her wealthy protector with such skill, with such calculation, with such efficient habits of physical practice, that she who thought herself ripe for adultery had long grown ready for harlotry." Thus, when a very distant young relative from the country comes to work for Dreyer, who tells the lad to call him Uncle, Martha sees in the boy "warm, healthy young wax that one can manipulate and mold till its shape suits your pleasure" and, once she has perceived her own lust, "no vacuum cleaner in the world . . . could instantly restore all the rooms of her brain to their former immaculate condition."

Thus, the role of Knave falls to the clumsy, bespectacled youth, Franz Bubendorf, an unlikely hero who breaks his glasses on his first evening in Berlin and therefore, in a city where "outlines did not exist, colors had no substance," goes to bed alone and masturbates without walking through or tasting "Berlin at the very hour of its voluptuous glitter and swarming."

Lest you wonder how such an unpromising lad will catch, let alone sustain, your interest, rest assured that, before long, he will be willingly seduced, *standing up*, by the voracious Martha, who, before baring her thighs to Franz for the first of many visits, produces a rubber and says: "Wait, wait a moment, my sweet. Look, you must put this on; I'll do it for you, you awkward brutal darling." Later, before allowing Franz a repeat performance in his bed, she rinses out what she calls his "macky" for him and slips it back on his "shortish but especially thick" member ("Fatty is greedy! Oh, greedy," she croons later). Franz belongs in any testimonial to Masturbators Who've Made Good, for he goes on to satisfy Martha (and vice versa) "twice in one hour three or four times a week." At the time of the month when Martha is "closed for repairs today," she tells Franz: "You can't touch me, but I can certainly touch you, and nibble you, and even swallow you whole if I want"—which she's been doing all along anyway.

After many such bouts, Martha perceives that while "she had arranged her life the way she wished" and denied her husband the romantic togetherness of tours to Ceylon or Florida, this was not enough: "She needed a sedentary husband. A subdued and grave husband. She needed a dead husband." What comes of her and Franz's scheming to murder Dreyer would leave both Balzac and Dreiser cackling under their cypresses, but it is yet another Nabokovian surprise.

Along the way, we are treated to several visits by Nabokov and his wife as thinly undisguised characters on "visits of inspection" as well as the author-as anagram: Blavdak Vinomori and Mr. Vivian Badlook . . . to chess metaphors . . . and wordplay: two German playmates on holiday named Schwarz and Weiss; a Berlin swimmer named Schwimmer, etc. . . . fairy-tale allusions ("She slipped and lost a slipper, which had happened already in another life") and mock turtles and, of course, butterflies.

Chess assumes more importance than mere metaphor in Nabokov's next, *The Defense*—first published in Russian in 1930 as *The Luzhin Defense*—Luzhin being its chess grand-master hero. The first time I read *The Defense*, in the columns of *The New Yorker* prior to American publication in 1964, its austerity kept losing me to the perfume and other aperitif ads that enveloped it until I gave it up. On my second try, in 1971, I went the route with the paperback edition, but neither enjoyed nor fully appreciated it. In 1974, however, shortly after my ten-year-old daughter had administered ten decisive defeats in a row to me on the chessboard, I gave *The Defense* one more try. This time, it worked wonders for me, so, for what it's worth, unless you are already a chess regular, I recommend a little immersion in the game immediately before tackling *The Defense*.

In the sequence of Nabokov's Russian novels, *The Defense* is a bold leap forward into obsession—the area he made his own in English with *Lolita* and *Pale Fire* many years later. As a terrifying chronicle of the life and death of an émigré grand master, who discerns the pattern of a malevolent chess game in every event, every kindness, every obscenity, and every bathroom tile that confronts him, *The Defense* reminds me of a celluloid Nijinsky dancing a magnificent flying leap out of an open window in a movie *Spectre of the Rose*. It is not surprising, then, that in his preface telling why *The Defense* had to wait nearly thirty-five years to appear in English, Nabokov alludes to a flurry of interest in the late 1930's by an American publisher who turned Nabokov off when he suggested replacing chess with music and making Luzhin into a deranged violinist.

The Defense is a nervous breakdown of a book—unnerving, but held in taut rein by the author's burgeoning, maturing talent. It has many marvelous Nabokovian scenes: most notably, in one five-page paragraph, a symphonic description of a chess match . . . a funny farce scene in which Luzhin's future father-in-law asks a casual, superficial question about chess and Luzhin badgers him with a detailed answer . . . and the search for a misplaced hotel room, which Nabokov reprised two generations later (and not nearly so well) in *Transparent Things*. Emigration (a theme ignored in *King Queen Knave*) recurs in *The Defense,* with special poignance when Luzhin's father returns home from a meeting of the Union of Emigree Writers at which he was the only one present . . . or when an elderly general asserts that "it was not Russia we expatriates regretted but youth, youth." (What an impact that quick repetition makes!). Alfyorov, from Nabokov's first novel, appears in a bit part here, and Nabokov himself is also visible at a party—as a beginning poet in pale flannel pants who held his head high, making his "large, mobile Adam's apple" noticeable. And, in the three-week Berlin visit of a girl friend from what is now Soviet Russia, it is Luzhin's young émigré wife who perceives a world-weary truth of emigration: "both here and in Russia people tortured, or desired to torture, other people, but there the torture and desire to torture were a hundred times greater than here and therefore here was better." (I might substitute the word "opportunity" for "desire.")

Surprisingly, *The Defense* is marred by just a few overbred sentences of the ilk that *The New Yorker* in general and Nabokov in *Ada* have formally enshrined as literary virtue. ("He just could not manage to force himself not to think of chess . . ." one such nine-liner begins. A shorter one ends: "And on the November day which this dream preceded Luzhin was married.") And, while the modern-day prefaces with which Nabokov has decked out his Russian-into-English novels are generally enlightening and amusing with their ritualized digs at Freudians, hack critics, and lip-readers, his foreword to *The Defense* should be skipped—at least until after the novel is read. For this particular preface is a conceit in which Nabokov wonders why readers should struggle with a dialogueless novel (which, it so happens, *The Defense* is not) "when so much can be gleaned from its Foreword" and calls our attention, in chess terms, to the last pages of chapter 4, where "an unexpected move is made by me in a corner of the board, sixteen years elapse in the course of one paragraph"—as though this had been a prodigious feat in either the 1930's or the 1960's! Readers are much better advised to experience the magic of the conjurer *before* he shows his hand.

The Eye (Soglyadatay), first serialized by an émigré review in Paris, 1930, and second-serialized by *Playboy* in Chicago, 1965, is a mystery story that strikes a minor chord right after *The Defense*. Though it bears the relationship of a riddle to a chess puzzle, *The Eye* is a trick that works in barely 100 pages, aided and abetted by a 1965 preface in which the author disclaims all intent to trick, puzzle, fool, or deceive the reader—and then, in the same paragraph, does so with a Nabokovian put-down:

> . . . only that reader who catches on at once will derive genuine satisfaction from *The Eye*. It is unlikely that even the most credulous peruser of this twinkling tale will take long to realize who Smurov is. I tried it on an old English lady, two graduate students, an

ice-hockey coach, a doctor, and the twelve-year-old child of a neighbor. The child was the quickest, the neighbor, the slowest.

More fairly, and just as accurately, Nabokov says that "the theme of *The Eye* is the pursuit of an investigation which leads the protagonist through a hell of mirrors and ends in the merging of twin images." Unlike his hero's identity, this aspect is implicit throughout —as when the narrator leaves a flower shop:

> As I pushed the door, I noticed the reflection in the side mirror: a young man in a bowler carrying a bouquet, hurried toward me. That reflection and I merged into one. I walked out into the street.

Despite its brevity, *The Eye* (watch that title and say it aloud, which is perhaps the most vital clue you'll find here) offers a couple of my favorite Nabokovian scenes. In one, a Berlin émigré bookseller named Vikentiy Lvovich Weinstock moonlights as a spiritualist and converses with Mohammed, Caesar, Pushkin, and Lenin! (Weinstock asks Lenin if he will talk of life beyond the grave, but Lenin prefers not to because he "must wait till there is a plenum.") In the other, in an émigré salon, Smurov tells the harrowing tale of his escape from Russia and his comeuppance at the Yalta railroad station—a narrative that is quietly punctured by another guest's remarking that Yalta doesn't have a railroad station. Who *is* Smurov? And, for connoisseurs of contemporary relevance, Smurov's supporting cast includes a fanatical diarist named Bogdanovich and a stolid jovial spouse named Khrushchov, who lives at 5 Peacock Street in the Russian quarter of Berlin and who "always overdoes his jokes"—such as, on Christmas Eve, donning his wife's fur coat and mincing around the room to general laughter, which gradually grows forced . . .

Glory (Podvig, meaning *The Exploit,* 1932), Nabokov's fifth novel, was the last to be issued in English (1971), and this bears perhaps his most self-satisfied foreword—in which he writes his own review to be appropriated by critics who *do* read beyond jacket blurbs. Nabokov's notice is, to no great surprise, highly favorable: *Glory* "soars to heights of purity and melancholy that I have only attained in the much later *Ada*" and there is even a reference to "mastertricks on the part of the wizard who made Martin." The foreword, much of which discusses Nabokov in the third person, happens to be illuminating as well as conceited, but it gives away so much that it is perhaps best read *after Glory.*

Martin is Martín Edelweiss and, though he is as pure and lofty as the Alpine flower whose name he bears, he represents Nabokov's most direct confrontation of the restless tragedy of emigration: a hero who lives the émigré dream, disappearing into the land he once fled to fulfill himself in what is now an alien void. Until that climactic moment, *Glory* is Nabokov's most autobiographical novel. (In fact, Nabokov admits that he once considered joining the remnants of the White Army to see if he could locate, somewhere in the Ukraine, the girl he calls "Mashenka" in *Mary* and "Tamara" in his autobiography, *Speak, Memory.*) *Glory* has whole sections that overlap Nabokov's own boyhood, his escape from Russia, and his studies at Cambridge. In his foreword to *Glory,* he admonishes us not to compare notes with *Speak, Memory.* The same three-foot model of a *wagons-lits* international sleeping car near the beginning of his novel opens chapter 7 of his autobiography, but Nabokov is right in advising us not to play this game. "The fun of *Glory,*" he writes, "is elsewhere. It is . . . in the echoing and linking of minor events, in back-and-forth switches, which produce an illusion of impetus: in an old daydream directly becoming the blessing of the ball hugged to one's chest, or in the casual vision of Martin's mother grieving beyond the time-frame of the novel in an abstraction of the future that the reader can only guess at. . . ." *Glory*'s appeal to this reader is that Martin Edelweiss is Nabokov's most appealing hero:

> Martin was one of those people for whom a good book before sleep is something to look forward to all day. Such a person, upon happening to recall, amidst routine occupations, that on his bedside table a book is waiting for him, in perfect safety, feels a surge of inexpressible happiness.

On the night in question, during a stayover in London, Martin's reading-in-bed of *The Lady With the Little Dog* is interrupted by a visit from his host's daughter—a pedantic tease named Sonia to whom Martin has long been attracted. Pleading fear, insomnia, and cold, Sonia climbs into bed with him. But, when Martin tries to take his comforting one stroke further, she bursts into prim English tears and flees his room most properly—only to pop back in long enough to call him "Idiot." The next morning, at breakfast,

Sonia's first words to Martin are: "I forgive you, because you are Swiss, and 'cretin' is a Swiss word, jot that down." And the irony of it is that the Greatest Single Truth about Martin and Sonia is that they are both Russian to the core of their transplanted beings.

Kamera obskura (in Russian, 1933) was published in a British translation (1936) as *Camera Obscura* and then revised in English by Nabokov for its American debut (1938) as *Laughter in the Dark,* which is the title it is known by now. *Laughter in the Dark* bears a surface resemblance to the later *Lolita*; it is, after all, about the blind, fatal infatuation of a middle-aging art critic with a teen-age movie usherette. But, to this eye, it marks the flowering of Nabokov the Victorian moralist—from its opening sentences—

> Once upon a time there lived in Berlin, Germany, a man called Albinus. He was rich, respectable, happy; one day he abandoned his wife for the sake of a youthful mistress; he loved; was not loved; and his life ended in disaster.

—to a rending, sentimental scene of moral retribution in which, after the heartless Margot has trapped Albinus Kretschmar into abandoning home and family for her, his eight-year-old daughter thinks she hears her father returning, throws open a window, and dies of pneumonia. This is barely halfway through *Laughter in the Dark* and not even this—on top of the shoddiest betrayals—turns Albinus away from his obsession with this hard-boiled bitch, evil beyond her years until, physically blinded after fleeing one of her many lies, he stalks her with a pistol in a drawing room she is looting . . .

The love scenes—or, rather, the lovemaking scenes—are as impassioned as any in *King Queen Knave,* but nowhere nearly as explicit: "Her nudity was as natural as though she had long been wont to run along the shore of his dreams. There was something delightfully acrobatic about her bed manners." Or: "He kept discovering new charms in her—touching little things which in any other girl would have seemed to him coarse and vulgar." But the ultimate Victorian touch is the irresistible hold on Margot of her first seducer, a satyric, satiric cartoonist named Axel Rex (though one is tempted to think of *Laughter in the Dark*'s blinded hero as Albinus Rex).

Like *King Queen Knave, Laughter in the Dark* has Germans, rather than Russians, in its triangles. A minor, though pivotal, character named Udo Conrad is presented, during a journey through France, as an émigré *German* writer, and there are even allusions to Mussolini and Nazi Germany, but the decadence that envelops Albinus—and of which he is part—is presented often in artistic metaphors. These range from patronizing ("Then, one night, as he was giving his learned mind a holiday and writing a little essay . . . upon the art of the cinema") to shockingly coarse, as when this philandering art critic writes a letter to his forsaken wife assuring her that he treasures her despite the Margot episode "which has bruised our family happiness as the knife of a madman slashes a picture." But, in an irony that Nabokov as well as the reader must cherish, the villain Axel Rex, who has dabbled in art forgery, recognizes some of his own masterpieces displayed on the art critic's walls under other identities.

There are a number of Nabokovian frills and delights in *Laughter in the Dark:* an actress named Dorianna Karenina who has never heard of an author called "Doll's Toy" or something like that . . . assigning the name of Albinus to a blond rabbit of a hero whose nose twitches beneath his big white . . . or *déjà vu* motif of doors . . . butterflies fluttering about in the early coolness after Albinus' first night with Margot . . . and, in his agonies of blindness, his awareness that, though his "specialty had been his passion for art, his most brilliant discovery had been Margot. But now, all that was left of her was a voice, a rustle and a perfume; it was as though she had returned to the darkness of the little cinema from which he had once withdrawn her."

Axel Rex is a monster—more Quilty than Humbert, one might say, but, ideally, *Laughter in the Dark* should be read as a proper Victorian novel, meatier than most, with just a hint of a wink from the author, as when Albinus tells Margot: "You know quite well, pussy—" and Nabokov interrupts their dialogue to announce: "He had gradually got together quite a little menagerie of pet names."

Nabokov wrote *Despair* in Russia in 1932 under the "far more sonorous howl" of a title, *Otchayanie*. The Russian version was serialized in Paris in 1934 and published in Berlin in 1936 and, in that same year, translated by Nabokov himself into what he considered "stylistically clumsy" English and published a year later by John Long, Ltd., of London. "Although I had been scribbling in English all my literary life in the margins . . . this was my first serious attempt (not counting a wretched poem in a Cambridge University review, circa 1920) to use English for what may be loosely termed an artistic purpose." For the 1966 American edition of *Despair*, he not only revamped the translation, but revised the Russian original.

Despite Jean-Paul Sartre's misplaced critical emphasis on its anti-hero's émigré roots, *Despair*'s Hermann is, in fact, a German of Russian descent who happens to harbor the most unrealistic, toadying, dumb-intellectual, parlor-pink sentiments among his deranged mental baggage. *Despair* begins in a nebulous Prague, where Hermann—a well-to-do, but financially failing, chocolate manufacturer—stumbles across a tramp he perceives to be his physical look-alike. Hermann concocts a plot to murder Felix the Tramp, palm him off on an unsuspecting world as a dead Hermann, and once his "widow" has collected the insurance, elope with her on Felix's passport. So insane is Hermann, a man who hates mirrors and will not have any in his home, that nobody else discerns the resemblance between him and Felix, dead or alive. Worse still, Hermann is so blind to all else but himself that he fails to perceive what his own words show the reader—that his wife is betraying him with her cousin Ardalion.

The double as mirror image, so implicit in *The Eye,* is rendered both explicit and distorted in *Despair.* Nabokov signals in his foreword that *Despair* possesses "something of the rhetorical venom that I injected into the narrator's tone in a much later novel. Hermann and Humbert are alike only in the sense that two dragons painted by the same artist at different periods of his life resemble each other. Both are neurotic scoundrels, yet there is a green lane in Paradise where Humbert is permitted to wander at dusk once a year; but Hell shall never parole Hermann." There are also, however, early-warning symptoms in *Despair* of the word diseases that erupted in *Ada*: " 'First,' said Ardor-lion to his fair cousin, a horrid tease, 'you should learn to spell my name.' . . . "No, that's not verse, that's from Dusty's great book, *Crime and Slime.* Sorry: *Schuld und Sühne* (German edition)" . . . "Finis. Farewell, Turgy! Farewell, Dusty!" And, since *Despair* is presented as Hermann's memoir of a perfect crime bollixed only by "the inertia, pigheadedness, prejudice of humans, failing to recognize me in the corpse of my flawless double," Hermann tends to harangue the reader like a Nabokov-within-a-Nabokov-novel or a Humbert-in-a-Hermann:

> If every now and again my face pops out from behind a hedge, perhaps to the prim reader's annoyance, it is really for the latter's good . . .
>
> Tum-tee-tum. And once more—TUM! . . . And a damned good fool I *have* made of someone. Who is he? Gentle reader, look at yourself in the mirror, as you to seem like mirrors so much.
>
> His name turned out to be Felix, "the happy one." What his surname was, gentle reader, is no business of yours.

I must admit that, for almost half of *Despair*, I was annoyed, if not repelled, by this obnoxious form of address. Around midpoint, however, I began to laugh at it, then with it, and, toward the end, I wound up loving it. The dawn of loving *Depair* will come to different readers at different places (and, for a few, not at all), but my magic moment came three-quarters of the way through—with this wonderful émigré spoof of Marxist-Leninist dialectic, ostensibly addressed by Hermann to Nabokov, alias V. Sirin:

> Having at last made up my mind to give my manuscript to one who is sure to like it and do his best to have it published, I am fully aware of the fact that my chosen one (you, my first reader) is an *émigré* novelist, whose books cannot possibly appear in the U.S.S.R. Maybe, however, an exception will be made for this book, considering that it was not you who actually wrote it. Oh, how I cherish the hope that in spite of your *émigré* signature (the diaphanous spuriousness of which will deceive nobody) my book may find a market in the U.S.S.R.! As I am far from being an enemy of the Soviet rule, I am sure to have unwittingly expressed certain notions in my book, which correspond perfectly to the dialectical demands of the current moment. It even seems to me sometimes that my basic theme, the resemblance between two persons, has a profound allegorical meaning. This remarkable physical likeness probably

appealed to me (subconsciously!) as the promise of that ideal sameness which is to unite people in the classless society of the future; and by striving to make use of an isolated case, I was, though still blind to social truths, fulfilling, nevertheless, a certain social function. And then there is something else; the fact of my not being wholly successful when putting that resemblance of ours to practical use can be explained away by purely social-economic causes, that is to say, by the fact that Felix and I belonged to different, sharply defined classes, the fusion of which none can hope to achieve single-handed, especially nowadays, when the conflict of classes has reached a stage where compromise is out of the question. True, my mother was of low birth and my father's father herded geese in his youth, which explains where, exactly, a man of my stamp and habits could have got that strong, though still incompletely expressed leaning towards Genuine Consciousness. In fancy, I visualize a new world, where all men will resemble one another as Hermann and Felix did; a world of Helixes and Fermanns; a world where the worker fallen dead at the feet of his machine will be at once replaced by his perfect double smiling the serene smile of perfect socialism. Therefore I do think that Soviet youths of today should derive considerable benefit from a study of my book under the supervision of an experienced Marxist who would help them to follow through its pages the rudimentary wriggles of the social message it contains. Aye, let other nations, too, translate it into their respective languages, so that American readers may satisfy their craving for gory glamour; the French discern mirages of sodomy in my partiality for a vagabond; and Germans relish the skittish side of a semi-Slavonic soul. Read, read it, as many as possible, ladies and gentlemen! I welcome you all as my readers.

Oh, what an East German academician Hermann would have made! And what a misfit Nabokov would have made (while he lasted) in Soviet Russia! Above all, what a paragraph of pseudo-hortatory prose!

If I have focused on politics here, it is appropriate because Nabokov's next, *Invitation to a Beheading* (published in Russian in 1935 as *Priglashenie na Kazn';* translated into English by the author and his son in 1959), was his first full-length venture into Allegoryland. Conceived between uprootings by Bolshevism and Nazism, *Invitation to a Beheading* has for a hero an exceptional everyman named Cincinnatus C., condemned to death for "gnostical turpitude," which, in his case, seems to be the crime of being opaque in a land or a world where everyone else must be transparent and where "that which does not have a name does not exist." Despite the hero's name, the world outside Cincinnatus' cell is a Russian landscape peopled by Rodions and Arkady Ilyiches. Two pages into the text, Cincinnatus C.'s jailer enters his cell and offers to waltz with him. Not long after, the prison director drops by to eat one of the condemned man's last meals for him. ("Excellent sabayon!") At his trial, we learn, the law required that defense attorney and prosecutor be uterine brothers, but, since such a pair were not available, two unrelated lawyers wore make-up to resemble each other. Welcome to the Nabokov-of-the-Absurd, wherein Cincinnatus C.'s friendly executioner informs him:

> ... "You bear an extraordinary resemblance to your mother. I myself never had the chance of seeing her, but [the prison director] kindly promised to show me her photograph."
> "At your service," said the director, "we'll obtain one for you."

The executioner then tells Cincinnatus:

> ..."Anyway, apart from this, I have been a photography enthusiast ever since I was young; I am thirty now, and you?"
> "He is exactly thirty," said the director.
> "You see, I guessed right."...

Until the allegorical *Bend Sinister* came along in English a dozen years later, *Invitation to a Beheading* might have seemed a departure from Nabokov's *oeuvre*. But—in its present form, at least—it is never a disconnection. Word games flourish here, too, as when Nabokov reminds his condemned man that "anxiety" consists of "tiny" and "axe." And, in this setting, instead of butterflies, we experience a moth the size of a man's hand and we see its "brown, white-dappled abdomen, its squirrel face, the black globules of its eyes and its feathery antennae resembling pointed ears." And to Nabokov's recurrent geometry of mirror images (*e.g.*, the executioner and the condemned man) is added an algebraic corollary of totalitarianism and politics (if not yet life and art)—that minuses times minuses make pluses.

At Oak Creek Canyon, Arizona, writing his 1959 preface to his *Beheading*, Nabokov observed that, two decades earlier:

> Emigre reviewers, who were puzzled but liked it, thought they distinguished in it a "Kafkaesque" strain. ... Spiritual affinities have no place in my concept of literary criticism, but if I did have to choose a kindred soul, it would certainly be that great artist rather than G. H. Orwell or other popular purveyors of illustrated ideas and publicistic fiction. Incidentally, I could never understand why every book of mine invariably sends reviewers scurrying in search of more or less celebrated names for the purpose of passionate comparison. During the last three decades they have hurled at me (to list but a few of these harmless missiles) Gogol, Tolstoevski, Joyce, Voltaire, Sade, Stendhal, Balzac, Byron, Beerbohm, Proust, Kleist, Makar Marinski, Mary McCarthy, Meredith (!), Cervantes, Charlie Chaplin, Baroness Murasaki, Pushkin, Ruskin, and even Sebastian Knight. One author, however, has never been mentioned in this connection—the only author whom I must gratefully recognize as an influence upon me at the time of writing this book; the melancholy, extravagant, wise, witty, magical, and altogether delightful Pierre Delalande, whom I invented.

Such a clue is likely to drive the Nabokov buff to the Petit Larousse, where he will find Descartes, but won't find Delalande. In any event, not only is Nabokov's executioner named M'sieur Pierre, but *Invitation to a Beheading* leads off with an epigraph in French from the legendary Delalande. Translated, it says: *"Just as a madman believes he is God, we believe we are mortals."*

Nabokov's ninth Russian novel, *The Gift (Dar)*, is the longest and most difficult in every respect—starting with the nearly two decades it took him to publish it properly in Russian! Written between 1935 and 1937 in Berlin and France, it was serialized in Paris by an émigré magazine, which, however, rejected the fourth of its five chapters—a literary biography that is the nucleus of *The Gift* —because of its intellectual frivolity: an event that also occurs in the third chapter and which Nabokov looks back on ruefully as "a pretty example of life finding itself obliged to imitate the very art it condemns." Only in 1952 did the Chekhov Publishing House of New York bring out a complete edition of *Dar* in Russian; not until 1963 was it published in English as *The Gift* and serialized in *The New Yorker*. Between the lines of this contorted publishing history —and in many lines of *The Gift*—one can detect much more cruelty, misery, and frustration than the more cheerful Nabokov of the 1970's would admit to.

The Gift is also the most difficult of all to fathom, unless you are steeped in knowledge and love (and, to some extent, linguistic comprehension) of much nineteenth-century Russian literature. In the foreword he wrote in 1962, Nabokov gives fair warning: "The world of *The Gift* being at present as much of a phantasm as most of my other worlds, I can speak of this book with a certain degree of detachment. It is the last novel I wrote, or shall ever write, in Russian. Its heroine is not Zina, but Russian Literature. The plot of Chapter One centers in Fyodor's poems. Chapter Two is a surge toward Pushkin in Fyodor's literary progress and contains his attempt to describe his father's zoological explorations." At the end of chapter 2, Fyodor changes Berlin lodgings and Nabokov concludes the chapter: "The distance from the old residence to the new was about the same as, somewhere in Russia, that from Pushkin Avenue to Gogol Street." This is his way of telling us that chapter 3 will shift to Gogol, though its real hub will be a love poem dedicated to the Zina he is about to meet therein. Chapter 4 is the fantastic literary biography of the nineteenth-century Russian social critic, Nikolai Gavrolovich Chernyshevsky (1828-1889), a revered and prophetic figure in Soviet Russia today, which is why even the objective Soviet *Who's Who* objected to Nabokov's "tendentiously distorted picture of N. G. Chernyshevsky." Though he was the antithesis of almost everything Nabokov would or could stand for, Chernyshevsky was blessed with scores of biographers, but few good biographies—and so, today, it is Nabokov's lampoon of his life inside a novel that gives Chernyshevsky any immortality he enjoys outside (perhaps even inside) Russia. In reading chapter 4, it is unnecessary and unwise to try to separate fact from fiction: when you do, you find that the likeliest pranks (such as a benign minister of justice named Nabokov) turn out to be true (the author's grandfather, Dmitri Nabokov, 1827-1904, was indeed minister of justice for eight years under two czars). Chapter 4 is not only what Nabokov modestly calls a "spiral within a sonnet," but a virtuoso feat of scholarship, imagination, prose, and poetry. It is a hard act to follow, but Nabokov manages a delightful chapter 5 (ornamented by critiques of chapter 4) which, in his words, "combines all the preceding themes and adumbrates the book Fyodor dreams of writing some day: *The Gift*. I wonder how far the imagination of the reader will follow the young lovers after they have been dismissed."

The answer for this reader is: "To the end of the book—and beyond!" For *The Gift* is the thick, old-fashioned, semi-Dickensian Russian novel many of us would dream of reading if we understood Nabokov's rich native tongue—and here it is in his own cotranslation (with Michael Scammell and, to a lesser extent, Dmitri Nabokov the Singer—the Son, not the Grandfather, the Minister).

Nevertheless, *The Gift* is the only Russian novel by Nabokov that I would not recommend to every reader. It can most safely be endorsed for the Nabokov buff—in particular, the one who cherishes *Pale Fire* over *Lolita*. For *The Gift* is immensely difficult—and the best advice I have for getting through it, *if* you find yourself having difficulty, is to go on reading it in sequence, but take a day off between chapters and look upon *The Gift* as five different novellas with overlapping characters.

By way of confession (I will have a more shameful one to make when we confront *Ada*), let me say that when I first started to read *The Gift* in 1971, I gave it up in revulsion halfway through the first chapter. Early in the action, a Berlin émigré namesake of Chernyshevsky calls the fledgling poet Fyodor to tell him there is a review of him as " 'such a brilliant phenomenon, and the poetic talent of the author is so indisputable . . .' You know what, I shan't go on, but you come over to our place tonight. Then you will get the whole article. No, Fyodor Konstantinovich, my good friend, I won't tell you anything now, neither who wrote this review, nor in what émigré Russian-language paper it appeared, but if you want my personal opinion, then don't be offended, but I think the fellow is treating you much too kindly. So you'll come? Excellent. We'll be expecting you." On his way over, Fyodor dreams a twenty-page bouquet of reviews, only to be greeted at the door by a newspaper containing nothing about him and the host yelping "The date! Go ahead, look at the date, young man!" It is April 1.

As one who still thought, at thirty-nine going on forty, that reviews meant recognition, I had so identified with Fyodor that I couldn't bear to go on. Three years older and wiser, but with every detail of that cruel hoax etched in my memory, I was able to reread those pages and go right on from there to be swept up into the tragic fate of the Berlin Chernyshevsky's son, who dies in a broken suicide pact . . . the revelation, in a beautiful passage at another salon, that Fyodor is the son of a famed adventurer who perished unexplainedly . . . the imagined conversation (that mostly took place) between Nabokov (Fyodor) and the poet-critic Khodasevich (Konchyev) . . . the émigré's embittered soliloquy against a typical Berliner who turns out, when he coughs with Russian intonation, to be a fellow refugee . . . chess . . . butterflies (Fyodor's father telling him "about the odors of butterflies—musk and vanilla; about the voices of butterflies; about the piercing sound given out by the monstrous caterpillar of a Malayan hawkmoth, an improvement on the mouselike squeak of our Death's head moth; about the small resonant tympanum of certain tiger moths; about the cunning butterfly in the Brazilian forest which imitates the whir of a local bird") . . . mirror images and executioners. As if that isn't enough to strike a responsive chord in veterans of *Invitation to a Beheading*, there is a vignette involving "the French thinker Delalande" at a funeral. Asked why he did not uncover himself, Delalande replied: "I am waiting for death to do it first."

Drained and limp, we put down *The Gift* and pause before rejoining the banquet. We contemplate the nine Russian novels plus the three American novels on which we have feasted, and we can now understand John Updike's rebuttal to Philip Toynbee who complained that Nabokov lacked heart. "The ability to animate into memorability minor, disagreeable characters bespeaks a kind of love," Updike wrote. "The little prostitute that Humbert Humbert recalls undressing herself so quickly, the fatally homely daughter of John Shade, the intolerably pretentious and sloppy-minded woman whom Pnin undyingly loves, the German street figures in *The Gift*, the extras momentarily on-screen in the American novels—all make a nick in the mind. Even characters Nabokov was plainly prejudiced against, like the toadlike heroine of *King Queen Knave*, linger vividly, with the outlines of the case they must plead on Judgment Day etched in the air; how fully we feel, for example, her descent into fever at the end. And only an artist full of emotion could make us hate the way we hate Axel Rex in *Laughter in the Dark*. Not to speak of towering creations like the father in *The Gift* and Dolores Haze." You, too, will have your favorite characters—one or two of whom will follow you around for life. Frankly, *Despair*'s Hermann rings me up from time to time in Vienna (just the other day, he tried to enlist my help in planting a news photo of a stork delivering a baby in the New York *Times*), and my wife, as a teacher of French who happens to parley-voo like a native, is every now and then meeting a visiting fireman like the French department head who wouldn't hire Pnin because he spoke the language. It is therefore almost impossible to disagree, at this point in our reading, with Updike's summing-up: "If we feel that Nabokov is keeping, for all his expenditure of verbal small coin, some treasure in reserve, it is because of the riches he has revealed. Far from cold, he has access to European vaults of sentiment sealed to Americans; if he feasts the mind like a prodigal son, it is because the heart's patrimony is assured."

Nabokov wrote several short poetic plays and a pair of longer dramas between 1922 and 1927 and then, a decade later, two more plays, *The Event* and *The Waltz Invention*. *The Event,* a dramatic comedy that has been described as a reversal of Gogol's *Inspector General*, was staged between 1938 and 1941 (for the most part obscurely) in Paris, Warsaw, Belgrade, and New York, and was perhaps the most successful play presented in the emigration, according to Andrew Field, who has read it in Russian and thinks that "in the hands of a brilliant and subtle director—say, an Alan Schneider—*The Event* could be enormously successful, but it is a play meant to be acted rather than read." Which is probably why it is not yet available to us in English. Its coeval, *The Waltz Invention*—which was being rehearsed for the Paris stage when World War II aborted its production—was made available to us in English three decades later (by Phaedra and then Pocket Books), and so it must serve as the dramatic intermezzo at our Nabokov banquet.

Admittedly, Nabokov's fable of a demonic, power-corrupted inventor named Salvator Waltz is the rather thin skeleton of an undernourished Shavian comedy (*Major Barbara* comes to mind) or even an allegorical operetta. Its action is written in the slightly stage-left manner fashionable in the 1930's and better exemplified by the W. H. Auden-Christopher Isherwood *Dog Beneath the Skin*; for example, act 2 features eleven old generals named Bump, Dump, Gump, Hump, Lump, Mump, Rump, Stump, Tump, Ump, and Zump, to which list Nabokov adds: "The last three are represented by dummies but differ little from the rest." And the most interesting dramatic character is an AC-DC reporter and adviser named Trance, who *"comes out of a closet. He may be played by a woman"*—or by the Joel Grey of *Cabaret.* Trance speaks such orgiastic lines as "Yes, yes, we believe you, as my former husbands used to say."

From mildly comic beginning to tepidly mystic ending, *The Waltz Invention* is not a play one can crusade for (or even call to Alan Schneider's attention), but the playwright had not given up hope. When he wrote, on December 8, 1965:

"When, sooner or later, *The Waltz Invention* sees the footlights and the black pit beyond, one hopes that whoever is going to produce it, and act in it, will take into account the poetry and the pathos underlying the bright demented dream. In contradistinction to the black pit of reality, the scenery should be as rich and verisimilar as a Dutch painting. Please, no damned fire escapes, garbage cans, skeleton platforms with actors in overalls standing on different levels. I want what Waltz wanted—real carpets, crystal knobs on the doors, and those sculptured armchairs upholstered in golden leather that he liked so much (he does not mention them, but I know). And the uniforms of the eleven generals must be beautiful, must glow like Christmas trees."

"The cradle rocks above an abyss, and common sense tells us that our existence is but a brief crack of light between two eternities of darkness." Clear the table for and open your mind (a *tabula rasa*, if you will) to a Nabokovian classic: his masterful autobiography, *Speak, Memory.* There are at least three ways to enjoy *Speak, Memory*—and no way not to enjoy this irresistible memoir:

... "I am going to show a few slides," he says at one point, and this approach is perhaps the best way, for *Speak, Memory* is autobiography in the form of a magic lantern show—and both magical and illuminating it is! Chapters 5, 6, 9, and 15 contain some of Nabokov's finest writing in any tongue: a loving portrait of Mademoiselle, his Swiss governess, and three passionate avowals of love for his butterflies, his murdered father, and his wife and son. Just sampling these highlights will incite you to . . .

. . . Read *Speak, Memory* straight through, from front to back, from cover to cover, the way books are still written and meant to be read. The reason this was not recommended right off the bat is that, like Nabokov's Russian novels, *Speak, Memory* is a compendium of serializations—and, in his usual long-after-the-fact foreword, Nabokov gives the odd publishing history of a book that started out in America as *Conclusive Evidence* in 1951 and reemerged a decade later as *Speak, Memory,* subtitled *"An Autobiography Revisited."* With extraordinary bibliographic zeal, he not only furnishes the titles, dates, and translators of its Russian, French, Italian, Spanish, and German editions, but also which chapter first appeared in French in 1936's second issue of *Mesures* and which appeared in *The New Yorker, Partisan Review, Harper's* or *Atlantic*. As a result, if this masterpiece has any flaw, it is that overlapping has not been sufficiently edited out. Thus, to cite just one example, the fate of some family jewels is reported toward the end of chapter 12 and then reiterated five pages later, at the start of chapter 13.

. . . For one who has read and relished the Russian novels, the third way to read *Speak, Memory*—much as Nabokov counsels against it in almost all his forewords—is what you will find yourself doing anyway: relating his life to his art. Chapter 12 is the real-life basis of his first novel, *Mary*, though Mashenka here is called "Tamara—to give her a name concolorous with her real one." Yet, there is more here than in *Mary*, because wrapped inside his words about the-girl-who-got-away is his lament for the-life-that-was-taken-away—and that is the meat of this tasty Nabokovian dish. It is implicit in his description of their correspondence during his family's flight that began in 1917—during which he notes that "for several years, until the writing of a novel relieved me of that fertile emotion, the loss of my country was equated for me with the loss of my love."

Elsewhere in *Speak, Memory,* one meets (however fleetingly) the Cambridge waitress Martin Edelweiss thought he'd impregnated in *Glory* and the revelation that *Laughter in the Dark*'s blinded adulterer, Kretschmar, was named as an act of revenge upon the first finder of a moth *(Plusia excelsa)* Nabokov thought *he* had discovered.

For an autobiography, *Speak, Memory* is laden with pranks and wordplays, but they are as blithe and harmless as butterflies. An essay on émigré writers, including a farcical encounter over a scarf with the Nobel laureate Ivan Bunin (who assured Nabokov: "You will die in dreadful pain and complete isolation"), is followed by the self-serving tribute: "But the author that interested me most was naturally Sirin. He belonged to my generation. Among the young writers produced in exile he was the loneliest and most arrogant one. Beginning with the appearance of his first novel in 1925 and throughout the next fifteen years, until he vanished as strangely as he had come . . ." Considering that Nabokov was Sirin

and Sirin was Nabokov, this ranks among Nabokov's more self-effacing mirror images.

Nothing short of reading *Speak, Memory* for yourself, however, can convey the joys on every page. A lovely episode on bedtime dawdling in boyhood ends with this plea: "I appeal to parents: never, never say 'Hurry up' to a child." Time marches on impressionistically: "A decade passed. World War One started. A crowd of patriots and my uncle Ruka stormed the German Embassy. Beethoven turned out to be Dutch." A life unfolds before us—sometimes on a chessboard or a spreading board—and a Russian childhood is remembered in such a dreamlike landscape of peasants and sleighs that even Nabokov remarks in wonder:

> Very lonely, very lonesome. But what am I doing in this stereoscopic dreamland? How did I get here? Somehow, the two sleighs have slipped away, leaving behind a passportless spy standing on the blue-white road in his New England snowboots and stormcoat. The vibration in my ears is no longer their receding bells, but only my old blood singing. All is still, spellbound, enthralled by the moon, fancy's rear-vision mirror. The snow is real, though, and as I bend to it and scoop up a handful, sixty years crumble to glittering frost-dust between my fingers.

But Nabokov has miles to go before we sleep.

Reading *Speak, Memory,* we *see* Nabokov living the Victorian existence—five bathrooms and hot-and-cold running tutors!—that other Victorian writers could only describe from the outside looking in. But, freed of the shackles and sodomies of that age and eventually deprived of its material comforts, only a nobleman in the finest (rather than the aristocratic) sense could write:

> My old (since 1917) quarrel with the Soviet dictatorship is wholly unrelated to any question of property. My contempt for the émigré who hates the Reds because they "stole" his money and land is complete. The nostalgia I have been cherishing all these years is hypertrophied sense of lost childhood, not sorrow for lost banknotes.

Though Nabokov apparently tells all in his foreword, it was not until the beginning of chapter 10—in a reference to "a ranch you and I rented"—that I realized *Speak, Memory* is addressed as well as dedicated to his wife, Véra. Subsequent references, among others, to living in "two shabby rooms with you and our child" and "the years are passing, my dear, and presently nobody will know what you and I know" confirm this device (which finds echoes in *Pnin* and, less successfully, *Look at the Harlequins!*). It may not be the tidiest form of literary presentation, but it does add a dimension of tenderness to a memoir that even Philip Toynbee (in *The Observer*) had to admit was "as brilliantly written as one would expect, but strangely human—even charming!—as well."

Nabokov and his wife and son, age seven, sailed for New York from St. Nazaire in the spring of 1940—and, a year later, *The Real Life of Sebastian Knight*, the novel he had started writing in English in Paris in 1937, was published by New Directions. Thus, *Sebastian Knight* is a significant milestone for Nabokov as well as a landmark for the student of his work. But, for one who has already read the later *Pale Fire*, it is a pallid rehearsal—an exercise in literary detection wherein both the prose and the detective are a trifle dense. Taking the form of the narrator's search for the truth about his dead half-brother, an author, *The Real Life of Sebastian Knight* is a bit overstuffed with synopses, excerpts, plot outlines, and writer's problems. To the poet Howard Nemerov, this was an inspiration:

> My admiration for the writings of Vladimir Nabokov began in college, when I read for the first time *The Real Life of Sebastian Knight* and thereon determined to spend my own more or less real life in writing Sebastian Knight's novels: *The Prismatic Bezel, Success* ("the probing of the aetiological secret of aleatory occurrences"), and most of all *The Doubtful Asphodel* ("A man is dying.... The man is the book; the book itself is heaving and

dying and drawing up a ghostly knee"). Of many reasons why I did not carry out this notable project, the best is that Nabokov, who had occupied the field first—immediately after inventing it, in fact—went on to write, if not those books, books very much like them, books about lonely, scholarly heroes a little insane, in situations more than a little absurd.

Nabokov's heroes, it has been noted more than once, are in themselves "methods of composition." But, even for the lay reader who cares only for his or her own reading pleasure (and more power to him or her in this electronic age!), *Sebastian Knight* has its charms and rewards. Chapter 6 is a delightful encounter between the dense half-brother and a self-serving, ax-grinding biographer of Sebastian Knight who didn't even know his subject had a half-brother and is determined to cover his traces at any cost to truth. Chapters 7 and 12 then emerge as hilarious putdowns of the kind of critical biography this book you're reading right now is a rebellion against: the kind in which the biographer, with preordained thesis in hand, berates or beautifies his subject on the basis of how he measures up to the biographer's thesis. In this case, what is stressed is "the fatal split between Knight the artist and the great booming world about him":

> Aloofness is a cardinal sin in an age when a perplexed humanity eagerly turns to its writers and thinkers, and demands of them attention to, if not the cure of, its woes and wounds. ... The "ivory tower" cannot be suffered unless it is transformed into a lighthouse of a broadcasting station. ... Now, Knight absolutely refused to take any interest whatsoever in contemporary questions. When asked to join in this or that movement, to take part in some momentous meeting, or merely to append his signature, among more famous names, to some manifest of undying truth or denunciation of great iniquity ... he flatly refused in spite of all my admonishments and even pleadings. ...

In the same oversignificant passage, the biographer even has the effrontery to pronounce Knight "hypersensitive (I remember how he used to wince when I pulled my fingers to make the joints crack—bad habit I have when meditating)." Oh, in the author of "The Tragedy of Sebastian Knight," ironically named Goodman, Nabokov has created a villain who could crack a pig's knuckle *(swininoga)* with Clare Quilty and put Kinbote into the shade of John Shade!

Try to envision the outrage such outrageousness would arouse in one close relative who has been left out of such a book and you will start to sense the appealing conceit of the anti-heroic half-brother's effort to set the record straight in *The Real Life of Sebastian Knight.* But, where it bogs down is in the synopses and scenarios that Nemerov and Nabokov both cherish perhaps too fondly. What, after all, can one say for *The Prismatic Bezel,* in which the murder victim is named G. Abeson and the unsuspected suspect is named Nosebag? Only that Nabokov and we have played word games together.

A similar mood—though a different set of reservations—applies here to Nabokov's next, *Bend Sinister* (1947). It is less humorous, more earthbound, less lofty than *Invitation to a Beheading* (1935)— and less polished than the earlier work. *Bend Sinister* starts off with the "fine writing" of a first novel—which, in a sense, it is: Nabokov's first novel written in America:

> An oblong puddle inset in the coarse asphalt: like a fancy footprint filled to the brim with quicksilver: like a spatulate hole through which you can see the nether sky.

A professor named Adam Krug went to school with the dictator Paduk in the city that is now Padukrad (as in Leningrad; note, incidentally, that the derivation of the title word "Sinister" is from "left," making *Bend Sinister* a turn to the left). A famous spa is now Padukbad (as in Marienbad, Carlsbad, etc.), during a time of upheaval, a gap in history. Krug's wife—under the care of a doctor named Krug—is dying in "a hospital bed (*gospitalisha kruvka*— again that marshland accent and he felt like a heavy crow—*kruv*— flapping against the sunset"), which is worth at least a hundred-krun note. (At this point, it may interest us to know that "Krug" means "tankard" or "jug" in German and "circle" in Russian.) Leaving the hospital for home, Krug crosses a closely-guarded bridge, but his pass is not honored by the guards at the other end because it was not countersigned by the other guards, who are illiterate—leaving Krug, for a while until the author rescues him, "doomed to walk back and forth on a bridge which has ceased to be one since neither bank is really attainable." Later, we meet a deposed, hunted baron hiding out in a "NOT WORKING" elevator, which he has made into a comfy den—until the elevator itself is carted away in a van with him in it.

Ember is a translator of Shakespeare who reversed the process and translated Krug's works into English with great success, about which he "felt abashed and apologetic and covertly wondered whether his particular brand of rich synthetic English had contained some outlandish ingredient, some dreadful additional spice that might account for the unexpected excitement." Between Ember and Krug, *Hamlet* is analyzed for many pages—its tale retold in chess moves and anagrams. ("Hamlet" is "Telemachus," son of Odysseus, alias Ulysses, minus "the unnecessary letters.") Or, to quote from *Bend Sinister: "Worte, Worte, Worte.* Warts, warts, warts." When Ember is taken into custody to bring pressure on Krug, the arresting officers are a tailored woman in a dove-gray suit and a man with a red tulip in the buttonhole of his cutaway coat—because a sensitive artistic soul must be arrested in high style.

A pre-Lolita maid named Mariette has "an inviting way of performing her household duties with nothing on to conceal her miserably young body save a dim nightgown, the frayed hem of which hardly reached to her knees. . . . Lovely ankles: she had won a prize for dancing, she said." Krug dreams that "he was surreptitiously enjoying Mariette while she sat, wincing a little, in his lap during the rehearsal of a play in which she was supposed to be his daughter."

And Adam Krug, the sanest (and therefore most dangerous) man in "Toad" Paduk's dictatorship, is addressed in palindrome as "mad Adam," though he is sane going and coming—even to the end when he is provoked into an insane, doomed attack on Paduk. The book ends with another view of the spatulate puddle which appeared after every rainstorm on the sidewalk near Nabokov's apartment on Craigie Circle in Cambridge, Massachusetts where he wrote *Bend Sinister.* In other words, his *Krug* has come full circle.

The book's most haunting pages concern the murder-by-mistake of Krug's son David, and Nabokov himself wrote, in his preface to the 1965 Time-Life reprint, that *Bend Sinister*'s "main theme . . . is the beating of Krug's loving heart, the torture an intense tenderness is subjected to—and it is for the sake of the pages about David and his father that the book was written and should be read." But these pages are few—and begin late in the book. What put *Bend Sinister* on my lesser Nabokov shelf are not just memories of *Invitation to a Beheading,* but "set pieces" that fizzle here: Krug's fifteen-page confrontation with Paduk and a faculty meeting with dialogue that reads like leftovers from *The Waltz Invention.* Nevertheless, *Bend Sinister* is a readable work of art in its own right—one that scarcely rates the Stalin Gothic badge and other decorations that Diana Trilling pinned on it in *The Nation* (June 14, 1947) when it first came out:

> . . . what looks like a highly charged sensibility in Mr. Nabokov's style is really only fanciness, forced imagery, and deafness to the music of the English language, just as what looks like an innovation in method is already its own kind of sterile convention. . . .
> On the other hand, to dismiss it simply as bad taste is to pass over a possible larger significance. Mr. Nabokov's novel is written in a claustrophobic style in which the reader's mind is allowed to do no work of its own, in which we are led by meaningless associations into blind alleys and trapped in boredom. But after all, Mr. Nabokov's story of the dehumanization of man under tyranny is a claustrophobic story. Whether or not it was the author's intention to model his prose system on the social system he is attacking, this is exactly what he has accomplished.

We take leave of lesser Nabokov and even lesser, unprophetic criticism and move forward through the texture of time to an age, a quarter of a century later, when Gilbert Highet (who once complained that Nabokov "despises us, his readers") is hailing him in the *Book-of-the-Month Club News* as "certainly the most original, the most tantalizing, the most unpredictable author alive," when the newest Nabokov *(Look at the Harlequins!)* is a Literary Guild selection, when those who failed to appreciate him at his best (who deplored *Lolita* and ignored *Pale Fire*) are hailing his worst and least *(Transparent Things)* as "a beautiful instance of Nabokov's mastery—deftly controlled, amazingly inventive, and finally poignant through all the complexities of its intellectual designs" *(Saturday Review)*. "The Lolita complex has engulfed the Italian cinema," writes *International Herald Tribune* critic Thomas Quinn Curtiss, reviewing a film called *La Bambina* that is the "forerunner" of "over a score of movies" in preparation concerning older men and girls under the age of consent. A City University of New York (CUNY) librarian named A. G. Mojtabai writes a first novel called *Mundome*, and the latest hyphenated critic of the New York *Times* hails her for coming "close to creating a genuine Nabokovian labyrinth, a verbal landscape whose ultimate standard of reality is itself alone." When D. M. Thomas, who fictionalized Freud in *The White Hotel*, publishes a 1983 novel, *Ararat*, it is hailed as "a homage to Nabokov" and "a Nabokovian novel," even though it is engulfed in many of the Freudian symbols Nabokov detested.

We are now in The Age of *Ada*. For *Ada* (1969) was when—on his seventieth birthday—Nabokov achieved best-sellerdom-*cum*-respectability. (He achieved both, but light years apart, with *Lolita*.) A turning point for him and perhaps a bend-away-from-the-sinister for the culture vultures who masquerade as the Literary Establishment, but a stumbling block for me. Here is the confession I have been hinting at throughout these pages: *every book discussed up to now has been read by me at least twice.* Sometimes, as with *The Defense* and *The Gift*, it took me two readings to begin to appreciate what I'd been reading. *But, with Ada, I detested her on first reading and dropped her on second reading,* after almost going the route again, but coming my ultimate cropper, four-fifths of the way through the book, on this sentence in the third paragraph of the crucial "Texture of Time" section:

> The 195 days preceding that event being indistinguishable from infinite unconsciousness, are not to be included in perceptual time, so that, insofar as my mind and my pride of mind are concerned, I am today (mid-July, 1922) quite exactly fifty-two, *et treve de mon style plafond peint.*

Those last seven words (according to "Notes to *Ada*, by Vivian Darkbloom") mean "and enough of that painted-ceiling style of mine"—and I had, indeed, had enough.

To some, *Ada* is nothing less than a whole history and rebirth of the novel—which must be, by nature, at least as incestuous as the lifelong love affair of Van Veen with his half-sister. *Ada* will keep scholars like Alfred Appel and Charles Kinbote and Blavdak Vinomori, the émigré Slavonicist, busy dissecting it for twelve times as long as it took Nabokov to write it—which means that, sometime in the twenty-first century, we may look forward to *The Annotated Ada,* and I will, G-d willing, be ready to tackle that tricky lady again. As Appel writes: "By thoroughly enjoying their caprices in *Ada*'s veritable bed of allusions, Nabokov's 'children of Venus' assume a literary life of their own."

Out of respect for the Cult of *Ada* as well as for Nabokov himself, I have loaded part 2 of this book with the most lucid and admiring critiques I could find that jibed with the book I was reading. But *Ada,* to *me,* marked the end of growth: the old magician playing tricks so tricky that he needed to append a glossary to explain them—or give them substance. The two novels that followed *Ada* have confirmed my fears.

Transparent Things (1972) was as tepid and tired as its anti-hero of "mediocre potency," Hugh Person (sometimes addressed as You Person), but it was not hard to read twice: short, smooth, well-built structurally and well-oiled mechanically, and just plain terrible both times. The second time around, I had fun chasing down the typographical flutter-by on which the hyphenated critic of the *Times* had built his entire review of the hardcover edition: a scene in which Hugh Person fears that "his wife was again feigning a feminine ailment to keep him away" and reminds himself that "he would have to consult an ophthalmologist sometime next mouth(sic)." To Christopher Lehmann-Haupt, "if one is to take Hugh's 'misprinting' of mouth as anything more than a joke—and it is usually risky to do so with Nabokovian jokes—then it is no more far-fetched to read it as Hugh's unconscious verbal slip (the associative cluster linking 'mouth' to 'female ailment' to menses to vagina dentata, and coming out 'mouth') than to take it as a reminder to see Nabokov's art as pure verbal patterns." Unfortunately, in the 158-page Crest paperback reprint that cost me $1.25, the significant typo (if that it was) wasn't there—or else mo*u*th had been miscorrected to mo*n*th.

Look at the Harlequins! (1974) is a livelier performance and, for all its faults, more fun than famine for one who has read this much Nabokov. It begins with this bibliography of *"other books by the Narrator":*

IN RUSSIAN:
Tamara 1925
Pawn Takes Queen 1927
Plenilune 1929
Camera Lucida (Slaughter in the Sun) 1931
The Red Top Hat 1934
The Dare 1950

IN ENGLISH:
See Under Real 1939
Esmerelda and Her Parandrus 1941
Dr. Olga Repnin 1946
Exile from Mayda 1947
A Kingdom by the Sea 1962
Ardis 1970

and its narrative is simply littered with references to "Sebastian—whoever that was" ... Dolly, whose boyfriend had just bought a new car, "a heavenly Hummer to go places with her" ... and "all my motels (*Mes Moteaux* as Verlaine might have said!)," including "the Lolita Lodge in Texas." And those of us who have made the descent from *Lolita* to *Look at the Harlequins!* or progressed in time from *Mary* to *Look at the Harlequins!* can't help enjoying the old dissembler's most incestuous mirror image yet: a narrator named Vadim Vadimovich who has a Doppelganger named Vladimir Vladimirovich. Toward the end, recuperating from a debilitating stroke, the narrator muses:

> ... Yes, I definitely felt my family name began with an *N* and bore an odious resemblance to the surname or pseudonym of a presumably notorious (Notorov? No) Bulgarian, or Babylonian, or, maybe, Betelgeusian writer with whom scatterbrained *émigrés* from some other galaxy constantly confused me; but whether it was something on the lines of Nebesnyy or Nabedrin or Nabldze (Nablidze? Funny) I simply could not tell. I preferred not to overtax my willpower (go away, Naborcroft) and so gave up trying ...

But even back in his unhealthy prime, Vadim Vadimovich was

> bothered that night, and the next and some time before, by a dream feeling that my life

was the nonidentical twin, a parody, an inferior variant of another man's life, somewhere on this or another earth. A demon, I felt, was forcing me to impersonate that other man, that other writer who was and would always be incomparably greater, healthier, and crueler than your obedient servant.

Good incestuous fun, but t'ain't art, Magoo! No matter, though, even if I have more fun wondering what the folks who were sold the Literary Guild and bought Nabokov in his self-dotage were making of all this. Whether or not they were willing to play Nabokov's games, let's hope they enjoyed him while he enjoyed himself. A year earlier, the poet-professor Paul Zweig (author of *The Heresy of Self-Love* and *Against Emptiness*) could profess with eloquence: "Not since Thomas Mann, or perhaps T. S. Eliot, has a writer bricked himself in so studiously. Perhaps that explains some of the enthusiasm he continues to evoke in his followers. Nabokov offers solace to those who have been unnerved by our indigenous free-lance anarchists of literature. (William) Burroughs, (Thomas) Pynchon, (Norman) Mailer, even (Saul) Bellow, dig in the underside of culture; they offer us literature as guerrilla warfare. Nabokov restores for us the tarnished but splendid ideal of art as a counter-institution, an oracular palace in which the reader can take refuge from the huns of contemporary vulgarity." I might not have gone this far, but I would certainly paraphrase Nina Berberova of Princeton, who said: *"If Nabokov is alive, it means that I am as well!,"* and echo her with a posthumous *"While Nabokov lives, art lives!"*

To eulogise the living and leave him with *Look at the Harlequins!* would be a disservice to Nabokov. There are other threads to pursue.

SHORT STORIES: Unburied treasures can be found in *Nabokov's Dozen,* (contains thirteen stories), *Nabokov's Quartet, Nabokov's Congeries,* and *A Russian Beauty.* Here, the translations from Russian are almost uniformly livelier than the ones created in English. The Russian Sirin was a freer, less inhibited soul than the more mannered stylist who wrote for *The New Yorker* and *The Atlantic Monthly* and, at short-story length, his vitality prevails. The translations are, of course, just as polished now as the stories that originated in English, but their movement and flights of fancy are wilder, more daring, more surprising, and more exciting. The one my soul will take to the grave is "A Visit to the Museum" (1939), which is every emigre recurrent dream and my own wishful nightmare ever since I was expelled from Prague. But other classics include: "Lik" (1938), a tale, set on the sunny Riviera, of an emigre actor in the shadow of death trapped by the reappearance of a bully from his Russian boyhood.... "An Affair of Honor" (1927): a man whose wife's apparent infidelity traps him into a duel he is mortally afraid of: complete with seconds named Marx and Engels (Markov and Colonel Arkhangelski) and the wheels of a train taking him to his doom and beating out the rhythm *"abattoir ... abattoir ... abattoir"* ... *"Spring in Fialta" (1938)*, a love story that Prof. Barbara Heldt Monter of the University of Chicago has called "as clear a masterpiece among Nabokov's short stories as *Lolita* and *Pale Fire* among his novels," and its English-language refugee phantom, " 'That in Aleppo once...' " (1943)... "First Love" and "Mademoiselle O" (both from *Speak, Memory* and "true in every detail to the author's remembered life") ... "The Vane Sisters" (1959), perhaps the most successfully diabolical of Nabokov's stories in English: in which Sybil Vane, jilted by her married lover D., writes her suicide note in her French mid-year examination booklet—

> *Cette examain est finie ainsi que ma vie. Adieu, jeunes filles!* Please, *Monsieur le Professeur,* contact *ma souer* and tell her that Death was not better than D minus, but definitely better than Life minus D.

and is dead by the time the teacher discovers it and phones her sister Cynthia. The story ends with a well-planted acrostic after Cynthia's death, though the teacher who narrates the saga of "The Vane Sisters" is "unaware that his last paragraph has been used acrostically by two dead girls to assert their mysterious participation in the story." The trick works, though it does not fully justify the conjurer's assertion (in his foreword to *Nabokov's Quartet*): "This particular trick can be tried only once in a thousand years of fiction."

POETRY: Nabokov's slim collection, *Poems* (1959), was out of print when, in 1970, McGraw-Hill issued *Poems and Problems,* containing fourteen English poems, thirty-nine Russian poems with English translations, and eighteen chess problems and solutions. Ten poems are included in *Nabokov's Congeries* (1968), later *The Viking Portable Nabokov,* a marvelous collection edited by Page

Stegner that also contains eleven short stories from *Nabokov's Dozen*, the complete novel *Pnin*, self-contained excerpts from *Despair, Invitation to a Beheading, The Gift,* and *Speak, Memory,* and essays and criticism that includes Nabokov's afterword to *Lolita*, his introduction to the 1965 reissue of *Bend Sinister*, his "Reply to My Critics" (most notably, Edmund Wilson), and various excerpts from his translations. The poems themselves are in a relatively minor key and, while F. W. Dupee in his *"The King of the Cats" and Other Remarks on Writers and Writing* (1965) calls Nabokov's long (five pages) poem, "An Evening of Russian Poetry" (1945), "great," I would cherish it simply as the wistful echo of a scream—

> Beyond the seas where I have lost a scepter,
> I hear the neighing of my dappled nouns,
> soft participles coming down the steps,
> treading on leaves, trailing their rustling gowns

—and enjoy it in tandem with the twenty-one-line "A Literary Dinner" (1942), in which the hostess-of-the-month (I mean, mouth) tells the poet "I want you to eat Dr. James" and he, being a good guest named Nabokov, obliges.

TRANSLATIONS: Reading his controversial *Eugene Onegin* is a wonderful way to read both Pushkin and Nabokov, for the Nabokovian commentary is two or three times the length of Pushkin's original. Nabokov's *Three Russian Poets: Translations of Pushkin, Lermontov, and Tiutchev* (1944) and *The Song of Igor's Campaign* (1960), translated from Old Russian, offer more conventional enlightenment. *Nabokov's Congeries* offers a fair sampling of *Onegin:* a sample translation of eight stanzas preceded by two excerpts from the Commentary: "On Romanticism" and "The Art of the Duel." The latter is nothing less than the death of Pushkin.

BIOGRAPHY: After his autobiography, *Speak, Memory,* any biography may seem redundant—but *Speak, Memory* ends in 1940 and there are many gaps before then. Therefore, Andrew Field's *Nabokov: His Life in Art* (1967) cannot be too highly recommended. Though mannered and over-stylized (people who write about Nabokov, present company included, are seldom immune to parodizing him), with such Russian affectations as "In Place of a Foreword," "In Place of a Bibliography," and even "In Place of an Index," and gushy to a fault, Field's biography is redeemed by its author's love for Nabokov and knowledge of Russian that has enabled him to probe the depths of everything Sirin ever published (some of which is still unpublished in English) and to read back numbers of *The Rudder* and other émigré periodicals. Nabokov once translated Hamlet's soliliquy into Russian and Field is one of the few scholars qualified to say that Nabokov's rendition "is the best there is in the Russian language" and transfer it literally back into an English that is not very far from what Shakespeare wrote:

> *To be or not to be: now this is*
> *The question: whether it is better for one's soul to*
> *endure*
> *The slings and arrows of furious fortune*
> *Or, against a sea of misfortunes having taken arms,*
> *To finish with them.*
> *To die, to sleep;*
> *No more; and if sleep ends*
> *The soul's melancholy and the thousand anxieties,*
> *Inherent in us—such a consummation*
> *One cannot but wish.*

Field then *shows* us how Nabokov gave Shakespeare an eloquence and poetry of his own in Russian without doing injustice to his English original. (Field even notes, parenthetically in connection with *Lolita*, that the last lines of Hamlet's soliloquy are: *"Nymph, in thy prisons/Be all my sins remember'd."*) He is a much more trustworthy critic of Nabokov-in-or-from-Russian than Edmund Wilson ever was. He is also especially good at analyzing *The Gift* and *Solus Rex*, an unfinished novel that was being serialized in Russian in Paris when France fell; *Solus Rex* is important as the seminal work that sparked *Pale Fire*. Field's critical biography also contains excellent synopses and analyses of Nabokov's plays and short stories, published and unpublished. His section on *Doppelgänger*s is strong and his "In Place of a Bibliography" is second to none in English. A newer volume by Field, *Nabokov: His Life in Part* (1977) is known to have caused all the Nabokovs terminal distress.

To reverse the Field, you might want to read Nabokov's 1944 critical biography, *Nikolai Gogol*, a wildly funny and Rabelaisian interlude written after (but published before) the similar biography of Chernyshevsky around which *The Gift* revolves. "The Government Specter," a chapter from Nabokov's book on Gogol, is available in *Nabokov's Congeries* if you want to sample it before seeking it out.

CRITICISM: Though Nabokov had published many critiques, few had been collected until *Strong Opinions* was issued in 1973.

Still, much of Nabokov's novels and almost all of *Ada* is literary criticism of a kind that he invented. As for criticism of and about Nabokov, the best sources are (in addition to Field's critical biography) Carl Proffer's *Keys to Lolita* (1968) and Page Stegner's *Escape into Aesthetics: The Art of Vladimir Nabokov* (1966), and, most comprehensively, the 384-page paperback Festschrift to which Northwestern University's *TriQuarterly* (published winter, spring, and fall) devoted its entire winter, 1970, issue (no. 17) in honor of Nabokov's seventieth birthday a few months earlier. Edited by Charles Newman and guest co-editor Alfred Appel, Jr., it is divided into four parts: Criticism (including Khodasevich on Sirin, Append Jeffrey Leonard and George Steiner [more or less] on *Ada*, Stanley Edgar Hyman on *Invitation to a Beheading* vs. *Bend Sinister,* and Nina Berberova on "The Mechanics of *Pale Fire*"); reminiscences (including Morris Bishop and Ross Wetzsteen on Nabokov at Cornell, Ms. Berberova and Lucie Léon Noel on Nabokov in the emigration, and Ellendea Proffer's enlightening report on "Nabokov's Russian Readers"); translators and translation (including Simon Karlinsky's *"Anya in Wonderland* Nabokov's Russified Lewis Carroll" and Carl Proffer's witty dissection of how Nabokov juiced up *King Queen Knave,* as well as contributions by Irwin Weil, Robert P. Hughes, and W. B. Scott); and, finally, tributes from a long list ranging from John Barth to John Updike, Anthony Burgess to Saul Steinberg, and R. M. Adams, holder of the Pan-American Chair for the Study of Overdeveloped Countries, to Timofey Pavlovich Pnin, Distinguished Visiting Professor Emeritus of Slavic and Baltic. It is also handsomely illustrated with photos by Phillippe Halsman and Horst Tappe and archive shots.

MIXED MEDIA: I have not yet seen Jerzy Skolimowski's film version of *King Queen Knave,* starring David Niven, Gina Lollobrigida, and John Moulder Brown in the title roles. If Stanley Kubrick's 1962 movie *Lolita,* is revived around your way, don't miss it—and that's even better advice if you've never read Nabokov; it is a fine film in its own right, even if it isn't very much of what Nabokov wrote for Kubrick. Even Nabokov has admitted (to Alvin Toffler) that "I thought the movie was absolutely first-rate. The four main actors (James Mason as Humbert, Peter Sellers as Quilty, Shelley Winters as Charlotte Haze, and Sue Lyon as Lolita) deserve the highest praise. Sue Lyon bringing that breakfast tray or childishly pulling on her sweater in the car—these are moments of unforgettable acting and direction. The killing of Quilty is a masterpiece, and so is the death of Mrs. Haze." ... The death of Quilty, in Nabokov's own words read by Nabokov, is also available on Spoken Arts record 902, *Lolita & Poems: Vladimir Nabokov,* and it is especially recommended for classroom both by Alfred Appel and *Scholastic Teacher.* The seven poems on side 2 include "An Evening of Russian Poetry," the raucous "Ballad of Longwood Glen," "On Translating Eugene Onegin," "Lines Written in Oregon," and one read in Russian.

And, finally, Alfred Appel, Jr.'s *The Annotated Lolita,* which is in a category by itself. Wherever your Nabokov-experiencing has taken you, it is advisable to come back every now and then to your high point of departure—be it *Lolita* or *Pale Fire, The Gift,* or *Speak, Memory.* Appel's *Annotated Lolita* offers a delightful way to revisit *Lolita.* Published in 1970 by Nabokov's new publisher, McGraw-Hill, it is the 1958 Putnam edition (with *its* errors corrected, but the same format and numbers for its 319 pages) flanked by 197 pages of preface, introduction, bibliography, and notes.

The Annotated Lolita, says Appel in his preface, "has developed out of my own experiences in teaching and writing about *Lolita,* which have demonstrated that many readers are more troubled by Humbert Humbert's use of language and lore than by his abuse of Lolita and law. Their sense of intimidation is not unwarranted; *Lolita* is surely the most allusive and linguistically playful novel in English since *Ulysses* (1922) and *Finnegans WakeCF184 (1939), and, if its involuted and constantly evolving means bring to mind any previous novel, it should be that most elusive of works, The Confidence Man* (1857) by Herman Melville."

Seven pages into the long introduction that follows Appel's short preface, we learn that "The transcendance of solipsism is a central concerning Nabokov." Tum-tee-tum. TUM! But read on, gentle reader—past the obligatory references to Beckett and Joyce, Raymond Queneau and Lewis Carroll, Dick Tracy and Bugs Bunny—and soon you, with perhaps a small "aha!" or two, will join Appel in identifying *Lolita*'s and Nabokov's motifs: *Doppelgangers* and mirror images . . . the play-within-the-play or work-within-the-work (Sebastian Knight's novels, the poem "Pale Fire," etc.) . . . fairy tales (from *Pale Fire*'s Zembla to *Ada's* Ardis) . . . colors . . . butterflies and metamorphoses . . . Nabokov's many, many references to and word games with Robert Louis Stevenson, James Joyce (Appel is most helpful with Nabokov's Joycean references, likes, and dislikes), and Edgar Allan Poe (Humbert's obsession was brought on by a boyhood misadventure with a nymphet named

Annabel Leigh, a few months his junior) . . . inevitably, solipsism (a philosophical theory that only the self exists or can be proven to exist) . . . and, lest we forget, McFate!

No Nabokovian theme, except perhaps his and his characters' recurrent insomnia, is given short shrift by McAppel. In pinpointing the other themes, he draws upon your reading plus his own readings in Russian literature to tell you what else each novel means to him. Thus, *"The Eye* parodies the nineteenth-century Romantic tale, such as V. F. Odoevsky's 'The Brigadier' (1844) . . . *Invitation to a Beheading* is cast as mock anti-utopian novel, as though Zamiatin's *We* (1920) had been restaged by the Marx Brothers. . . . Pnin's departure at the end mimics Chichikov's orbital exit from *Dead Souls* (1842), just as the last paragraph of *The Gift* conceals a parody of a Pushkin stanza"—not all of which you need to know to enjoy Nabokov.

Once you are no longer bogged down in Appel pandowdy and are back into *Lolita*, the familiar but delightful experience will achieve a new dimension with a little help from the rear, where Appel's annotations abound. In note 6/9 (page 6, annotation 9) we learn that " 'Vivian Darkbloom' is Clare Quilty's mistress" and are reminded that she is also "an anagram of 'Vladimir Nabokov.' " In a note nearly a page long, we also learn that 'Cue' is also the cognomen of Clare Quilty" and then we are also asked rhetorically:

> But who is Quilty?—a question the reader will surely ask (see the Introduction, pp. xiii-lxviii, and 33/9). As with H. H. and Lolita (*nee* Dolores Haze), Quilty's name lends itself to wordplay by turns jocose (see 225/1) and significant, since H. H. suggests that Clare Quilty is clearly guilty. Clare is also a town in Michigan (see 161/1), and, although Nabokov did not know it until this note came into being, Quilty is a town in County Clare, Ireland, appropriate to a verbally playful novel in which there are several apt references to Joyce. See 6/11.

Thanks for the geography lesson, Appel; don't know where McNab would be without you. Still, it *is* news that *fascinumCF184 is Latin for "a penis of ivory used in certain ancient erotic rites" (21/7), but not that the Metro is the Paris subway (22/5). It is good to know that the corpuscles of Krause* are "minute sensory particles occurring in the mucous membrane of the genitalia" (62/2) and fun to hear that one of the "invisibles" who serenaded Lolita from the jukeboxes of roadside America, Peggy Lee, was born Norma Egstrom (150/1), but perhaps not necessary to know, when a pocket diary is identified by Humbert Humbert as a "product of the Blank Blank Co., Blankton, Mass.," that "there is no such town" (42/6). There follows a long-paragraph dissertation on diaries in Nabokov's *oeuvre,* which, however, omits my favorite (from *Sebastian Knight*) characterization of a diary as "a poor method of self-preservation." And, since both Humbert and Appel reiterate that *Lolita* was written for the twenty-first century reader who might not have experienced its 1947-1952 background, there is a more serious omission when a passing line on page 160 goes unannotated: *"The Bearded Woman read our jingle and now she is no longer single."* A sentence or two in the next edition, please, Prof. Applejack, about the Burma-Shave billboards of our boyhood! But thanks for explaining Humbert's reference to:

> 173/3 *orchideous masculinity:* belonging to the natural order of plants akin to genus *Orchis.* Its Greek entymology adds a comic dimension, for *orchis* means "testicle" as well as the plant . . .

and for P.O.inting out that Humbert's two mail-drops along his roadside odyssey, P.O. Wace and P.O. Elphinstone, spell out P.O.W. (an allusion to Lolita's captivity) and P.O.E. (224/1). I don't think you handled "the township of Soda, pop. 1001" as sparklingly as you might have in note 222/2, though you did point out the fairy-tale significance of 1001.

You get around, eventually, to defining, but not elaborating upon, two of the recurrent words in all of Nabokov's books—"crepitate" (to crackle) and "nictitate" (to wink). There are also "micturate" (to piss) and "cuddity" (essence). But perhaps *The Annotated Lolita*'s most valuable service, for those who don't parley-voo, is the scrupulous translation of Humbert's frequent French—making this *Lolita* some five thousand words longer and many times funnier.

Appel's *Annotated Lolita* is, above all, a labor of love as well as scholarship—and one of its unadvertised rewards is a rare glimpse of Nabokov the Man in note 263/4. The reader may not have realized that The Enchanted Hunters hotel—where Lolita first seduced Humbert while Quilty lurked in a nearby john—was "restricted" against Jews, though one might have guessed it when there was no room at the inn for Professor "Hamburg" or "Humberg," but a space could be found for a Humbert. On page 263, the hotel's ad that it is "NEAR CHURCHES," but accepts "NO DOGS," prompts Appel to wonder

> ... if the hotel's policy of "NO DOGS" had been broken to accommodate Christian dogs, because "NEAR CHURCHES" was commonly used (c. 1940-1960) as a code sign, a discreet indication that only Gentiles were accepted ... "Refugee" H. H. is often mistaken for a Jew; see p. 81, where John Farlow is on the point of making an anti-Semitic remark and is interrupted by sensitive Jean. Quilty thinks H. H. may be a "German refugee," and reminds him, "This is a Gentile's house, you know" (299/2).*
>
> Nabokov's father was an outspoken foe of anti-Semitism. He wrote "The Blood Bath of Kishinev," a famous protest against the 1903 pogrom, and was fined by the Tsarist government for the fiery articles he wrote about the Beiliss** trial (Maurice Samuel mentions him several times in his book on the Beiliss case, *Blood Accusation* (1966)—coincidentally published at the same time as Bernard Malamud's novel based on it, *The Fixer*—quotes from Nabokov's reportage). Nabokov *fils* is also outraged by anti-Semitism, and, because his wife is Jewish, is sensitive to it in a most acutely personal way ...

---

*Subsequent to Appel's annotating *Lolita*, Nabokov has published *Look at the Harlequins!* in which his befuddled *Doppelgänger*, Vadim Vadimovich, is accused at Orly airport of having written an obscene book "about little Lola or Lotte, whom some Austrian Jew or reformed pederast rapes after marrying her mother.... To which Vadim, author of a Book-of-the-Decade selection called *A Kingdom by the Sea* about a nymphet named Ginny (Poe married his cousin, Virginia Clemm, when she was only thirteen, retorts   "You are talking of some other book altogether."

**Shortly before World War I, in one of czarist Russia's most bizarre court trials, Mendel Beiliss was acquitted in Kiev on a charge of ritual murder of a child.

And then Appel tells of Nabokov going with his son and his son's friend to a New England inn where, upon opening the menu, they noticed the succinct stipulation "Gentiles Only."

Nabokov summoned the waitress and asked her what the management would do if, right then, there appeared at the inn a bearded, robed man leading a mule bearing his pregnant wife—all three of them dusty and tired from a long journey.

"What—what are you talking about?" the waitress wondered.

"I am talking about Jesus Christ!" said Nabokov, pointing to the offending phrase, rising from his chair, and leading his party out of the restaurant. "My son was very proud of me," Nabokov told Appel.

4
BIBLIOGRAPHY: "THE PALLIATIVE OF ARTICULATE ART"

How to Use This Bibliography: Numbers atop most titles are Library of Congress call numbers. They are useful not only in libraries that classify books accordingly, but also for the reader who wishes to ascertain, by contacting the Library of Congress, whether or not a certain book is on its shelves in Washington or what libraries elsewhere in the U.S. have it.

Numbers in bold face are Dewey decimal classifications for finding book on many library shelves. Dewey decimal numbers vary from library to library, but the numbers herein should provide you with the basic codes that will help you find specific or related works in most libraries that use the system, though it is wisest to consult a library's own card catalog. *Warning:* Fiction is usually *not* classified by the Dewey decimal system. A Nabokov novel can usually be found under Fiction (N or NAB). Biographical works are often classified by libraries, not under Dewey decimal number 920 (biography) but under B (NAB), etc.

Some books—particularly those published abroad and a few (believe it or not!) overlooked by the Library of Congress—have not been cataloged at press time. Other numbers sometimes appearing are International Serial Book Numbers (ISBN) and Library of Congress card catalog numbers. Some details, such as new editions and paperback reprints and prices where listed, are subject to frequent change.

Additional quotations as well as comments by the author, editors, bibliographers or others are italicized.

A. BY NABOKOV, VLADIMIR VLADIMIROVICH, 1899-1977
(Alphabetically, by title)

"*The Nabokov bibliography is full of traps and obscurities. But it seems established that he has produced original work in at least three languages. I say 'at least' because . . . one story, 'O.,' taken up in* Speak, Memory *(1951) and later in* Nabokov's Dozen *(1958), first appeared under the same title, in French, in* Mesures *(Paris, 1939)."*
—George Steiner in *TriQuarterly.*

1. FICTION, POETRY, COLLECTIONS

PS3527.A15 A65 and PZ3.N121 Ad
Ada; or, Ardor: a family chronicle. New York, McGraw-Hill, and

London, Weidenfield & Nicolson, 1969, 589 p., incl. genealogical table. Subsequent paperbacks by Fawcett World (Crest P1409) and Penguin (14 003052 2). 813'.5'4. 71-79763 and 72-461541.

Anniversary Notes: See Appel and Newman, *Triquarterly* Festschrift, Section B of this bibliography.

Annotated Lolita — See LOLITA

PS3527.A15B4/1981
Bend sinister. New York, Holt, 1947, 242 p. Reissued in the Time Reading Program, New York: Time-Life Books, Time, Inc., 1965, and again in 1981 (in deluxe and paperback editions). *The Time-Life editions have an important 1965 introduction by the author.* 813 .5'4'19. 47-3534 and 81-1594.

Camera Obscura: See LAUGHTER IN THE DARK

PZ.N121Dc in English and PG3476.N3Z24 Rare Bk. Coll. in Russian, 1930
The defense. Translated by Michael Scammell in collaboration with the author. New York, Putnam, 1964, 256 p. Paperbacks by Capricorn (316) and Panther. Translation of *Záshcita Luzhina* (The Luzhin Defense), 1930. Cloth and paperback reprints in Russian: Ann Arbor, Ardis, 1979. 64-13017.

PG3476.N308 Rare Bk. Coll. (original, in Russian)
PG3476.N3083/1937 Rare Bk. Coll. (early British edition)
PZ3.N121 De2 (revised English translation)
Despair. by Vladimir Nabokoff-Sirin; translated from the Russian, *Otchayanie* (1931) by the author. London, J. Long, Ltd. 1937, 286 p. Despair, a novel by Vladmir Nabokov, translated and revised by the author. New York, Putnam, and London, Weidenfeld & Nicolson, 1966, 222p. Paperbacks by Capricorn (317) and Panther (586 02841 2). Cloth and paperback reprints of the Berlin 1931 edition in Russian: Ann Arbor, Ardis, 1978. 65-20683.

PZ3.N121Dg, PG3476.N3, and PG3476.N3 B4
Details of a Sunset and other stories. New York, McGraw-Hill, 1976, 179 p. Contains: Details of a Sunset. A bad day. Orache. The return of Chorb. The passenger. A letter that never reached Berlin. A guide to Berlin. The doorbell. The thunderstorm. The

reunion. A slice of life. Christmas. A busy man. **891.7'3'42.** 75-34086.

English-Russian Dictionary of Nabokov's Lolita: See LOLITA

PZ3.N121Ey (English) or PGR2905.A15 A2 50 (Russian)
The eye. Translated by Dmitri Nabokov in collaboration with the author. New York, Phaedra, 1965, and London, Weidenfeld & Nicolson, 1966, 114 p. Panther paperback 24530. Translation of *Sogliadatai.* (serialized in 1930). Cloth and paperback reprints in Russian of *Sogliadatai* also contain 12 short stories: Ann Arbor, Ardis, 1978, 252 p.

PG3476.N3A23/1979
Five novels by Vladimir Nabokov, with an introduction by Peter Quennell. London, Collins, 1979, 1,084 p. (Collins collector's choice). Contains: Lolita; The gift; Invitation to a beheading; King, Queen, Knave; Glory. **891.73 42 19.** 80-489397.

PZ3.N121 Gi (English) or PG3476.N3D3 (Russian)
The gift. Translated by Michael Scammell with the collaboration of the author. New York, Putnam, and London, Weidenfeld & Nicolson, 1963, 378 p. Capricorn paperback (318). Translation of *Dar* (incompletely serialized in 1937) first published in complete form in Russian: New York, Chekhov Publishing House, 1952. Paperback reprint of the complete edition: Ann Arbor, Ardis, 1975. 63-9667.

PZ3.N121 Gl (English) or PG3476.N3P6 (Russian)
Glory. Translated by Dmitri Nabokov in collaboration with the author. New York, McGraw-Hill, and London, Weidenfeld & Nicolson, 1972, 205 p. Paperbacks by Fawcett Crest (M1788) and McGraw-Hill (in 1980). Translation of *Podwig* (1932). Cloth and paperback reprints of the original Berlin edition in Russian: Ann Arbor, Ardis, 1974. **891.73'42.** 73-165256 and 80-15205.

PZ3.N121 In (English) or PG3476.N3P7 (Russian)
Invitation to a beheading. Translated by Dmitri Nabokov in collaboration with the author. New York, Putnam, 1959, and London, Weidenfeld & Nicolson, 1960, 223 p. Paperbacks by Capricorn (255) and Penguin (no. 1964). Translation of *Priglashenie na kazn'* (1938). Cloth and paperback reprints of the 1938 edition in Russian: Ann Arbor, Ardis, 1979. **891.73'42.** 59-11024.

PZ3.N121 Ki (English) or PG3476.N3K6 (Russian)
King, queen, knave. Translated by Dmitri Nabokov in collaboration with the author. New York, McGraw-Hill, and London, Weidenfeld & Nicolson, 1968, 272 p. Paperbacks by Fawcett Crest (T1287) and Panther (586 03319 X). Translation of *Korol,' dama, valet* (1928).Facsimile edition of Russian original: New York, McGraw-Hill, 1969. Cloth and paperback reprints of Russian original: Ann Arbor, Ardis, 1979. **891.7'3'42.** 68-22764 (English) and 70-82520 (Russian).

PZ3.N121 Lau and PS3527.A15 L3/1938 (in English)
PG3476.N3K3 (in Russian)
Laughter in the Dark, by Vladimir Nabokoff (sic), translated by the author. Indianapolis and New York, Bobbs-Merrill, 1938, 292 p. New York, New Directions, 1960, and London, Weidenfeld & Nicolson, 1961. Paperbacks by Signet (in 1950; out-of-print), Berkley Medallion, and Penguin. An earlier translation by Winifred Roy was entitled Camera Obscura: London, John Long, 1936. The 1932 original in Russian was called *Kamera obskura* and was reprinted in cloth and paperback in Ann Arbor by Ardis in 1979. **891.73.** 38-11644.

PZ3.N121 Lo (English) and PS3527.A15L617 (Russian)
Lolita. Paris, Olympia Press, 1955 (in English). *The notorious original, in two volumes, with many typos, has Library of Congress number 56-24827.* New York, Putnam, 1958, and London, Weidenfeld & Nicolson, 1959, 319 p. *"This edition of LOLITA is published by special arrangement with THE OLYMPIA PRESS."* Subsequent paperbacks by Crest, Berkley, and Capricorn. Other reprints: Franklin Center, PA, Franklin Library, 1979, and New York, Greenwich House, 1955. Translated by the author into his native Russian: New York, Phaedra Publishers, 1967, 304 p., in hard- and soft-cover editions; reprinted, Ann Arbor, Ardis, 1976, in paperback. **813'.5'4'19.** 58-10755.

PN1997.L66N3/1974
Lolita: a screenplay by Vladimir Nabokov (for the 1962 Stanley Kubrick film). New York, McGraw-Hill, 1974, 213 p. **812'.5'4.** 73-15918

PZ3.N121 An
The annotated Lolita, by Vladimir Nabokov, Edited, with pref., introd., and notes by Alfred Appel, Jr. New York, McGraw-Hill, 1970, 441 p. In hard- and soft-cover editions. *For one who will use it often, the more expensive hard-cover is favored over the trade paperback, which is poorly bound.* **813'.5'4.** 75-95819.

PS3527.A15L634
An English-Russian Dictionary of Nabokov's Lolita, by Alexander D. Nakhimovsky and V.A. Paperno. Ann Arbor, Ardis, 1982, 140 p. In cloth and paperback editions. *"Nabokov's Russian Lolita is a rare example of an author's translation of his own book into his own native language. Nabokov was also a major theorist of translation, and this dictionary codifies his own practice, listing every word and idiom in* Lolita *which is translated into Russian not in the way prescribed by the two major English-Russian dictionaries (Smirnitsky, Oxford)."*
813'.5'4 19 82-11645.

PZ3.N121LP and PS3527.A15
Look at the harlequins! New York, McGraw-Hill, 1974, and London, Weidenfeld & Nicolson, 1975, 253 p. **813'.5'4.** 74-10677 and 76-359789.

PZ3.N121 Mar (English) and PG3476.N3M3 (Russian)
Mary. Translated by Michael Glenny in collaboration with the author. New York, McGraw-Hill, 1970, and London, Weidenfeld & Nicolson, 1971, 114 p. Paperbacks by Fawcett Crest (M1602), Penguin, and McGraw-Hill (in 1981) Translation of Nabokov's first novel, *Mashenka* (1926). Cloth and paperback editions of the original 1926 Berlin edition in Russia: Ann Arbor, Ardis, 1979. **89 1.7'3'42.** 71-126749.

PS3527.A15A6
Nabokov's congeries. Writings by Vladimir Nabokov selected, with a critical introduction, by Page Stegner. New York, Viking, 1968, 536 p. Paperback edition: The Viking Portable Nabokov, New York, Penguin, 1978. Contains the complete *Pnin,* plus excerpts from *Despair, The Gift, Invitation to a Beheading,* and *Speak, Memory;* 11 short stories; 10 poems; essays, and criticism. **818'.5'209** and **813'5'4** 68-22868 and 77-14926.

PZ3.N121 Nab and PS3527.A15
Nabokov's dozen: a collection of thirteen stories. Garden City, NY, Doubleday, 1958, 214 p. Freeport NY, Books for Libraries Press, 1969. Franklin Center PA, Franklin Library, 1977. Also in Avon paperback (Bard 15354). Contains: Spring in Fialta. A forgotten poet. First love. Signs and symbols. The assistant producer. The aurelian. Cloud, castle, lake. Conversation piece, 1945. "That in Aleppo once . . ." Time and ebb. Scenes from the life of a double monster. Mademoiselle O. Lance — and a bibliographic note that ends, ". . . I am no more guilty of imitating 'real life' than 'real life' is responsible for plagiarizing me." **813'.5'4.** 75-91138.

PZ3.N121 Nab or Qar
Nabokov's quartet. New York, Phaedra, 1966, and London, Weidenfeld & Nicolson, 1967, 104 p. British paperback by Panther. Contains: An affair of honor, Lik, and The visit to the museum, all three translated by Dmitri Nabokov, and The Vane sisters, written in English. 66-28101 and 67-107171.

PZ3.N121 Ni
Nine stories. New York, New Directions, 1947, 126 p. **052'.** 47-12492.

PZ3.N121 Pal
Pale Fire: a novel. New York, Putnam, 1962, and Perigee Books, 1980, 315 p. Paperbacks by Berkley Medallion and Penguin: Russian translation by Alexei Tsvetkov: Ann Arbor, Ardis, 1980, 280 p. cloth and paperbound. ISBN 0-88233-602-9. **813'.54.** 62-7351 and 79-26742.

PZ3.N121 Pn or PS3527.A15P59/1982
Pnin. Garden City NY, Doubleday, 1957, and Cambridge, MA, R. Bentley, 1982, 191 p. Paperback by Avon (Bard 15800). Also contained in *Nabokov's congeries*. **813'.5'4 19.** 57-6299 and 82-1208.

PS3527.A15P6 (Rare Bk. Coll.)
Poems. Drawings by Robin Jacques. Garden City NY, Doubleday, 1959, 43 p. **891.7142.** 59-10681.

PG3476.N3A17
Poems and problems. New York, McGraw-Hill, 1970, and London, Weidenfeld & Nicolson, 1972, 218 p. Paperback by McGraw-Hill, 1981. Contains: 39 poems in Russian with

English versions by the author, 14 poems written in English, and 18 chess problems and solutions. **891.7'1'42.** 77-143446 and 81-8325.

PG3476.N3G6 Rare Bk. Coll.
Gornii put, *one of the earliest collections of poems by V. Sirin (alias Nabokov),* 1923, 180 p., *can be read in Russian at the Library of Congress.*

Portable Nabokov: See NABOKOV'S CONGERIES

PZ3.N121 Re
The real life of Sebastian Knight. Norfolk CT, New Directions, 1941, reissued 1959, 205 p. London, Edition Poetry, 1945. British paperback by Penguin. 42-2424.

PZ3.N121 Ru or PG3476.N3 A25
A Russian beauty and other stories, translated by Dmitri Nabokov and Simon Karlinsky in collaboration with the author. New York, McGraw-Hill, and London, Weidenfeld & Nicolson, 1973, 268 p. 72-10094.

Spring in Fialta — a volume of short stories published in paperback (now out-of-print) by Popular Library (1959) in English. The contents now can be found in other volumes of Nabokov stories. For Russian edition (1956), see VESNA V FIAL'TE.

PG3476.N3A17/1979 (in Russian only)
Stikhi. with an introduction by Véra Nabokov. Ann Arbor, Ardis, 1979, 320 p., in cloth and paperback. *"The first completely new edition by Ardis of Nabokov's work. Nabokov himself collected the poems for this volume, many of which were available only in rare émigré periodicals. Some are published here for the first time. It represents the most extensive publication of Nabokov's verse in over fifty years, and the only major collection covering his whole career."*
79-373291.

PZ3.N121 Tr
Transparent things. New York, McGraw-Hill, 1972, and London, Weidenfeld & Nicolson, 1973, 104 p. Paperback by Fawcett Crest (P2035). **813'.5'4.** 72-3989.

PZ3.N121 Ty or PG3476.N3
Tyrants destroyed and other stories. New York, McGraw-Hill, and London, Weidenfeld & Nicholson, 1975, 238 p. Contains 12 stories translated from Russian by Dmitri Nabokov: Tyrants destroyed. A nursery tale. Music. Lik. Recruiting. Terror. The Admiralty spire. A matter of chance. In memory of L. I. Shigaev. Bachmann. Perfection. Vasily Shishkov. And a 13th written in English: The Vane sisters. **891.7'3'42.** 74-19209 and 76-361599.

PG3476.N3V4 (in Russian only)
Vesna v Fial' te i drugie rasskazy (**Spring in Fialta and Other Stories**). 1956 Russian edition reprinted in cloth and paperback: Ann Arbor, Ardis, 1978. ISBN 0-88233-383-6. 57-24088.

PG3476.N3V6 (in Russian only)
Vozraschenie Chorba (**The Return of Chorb**). Stories and poems. 1930 Berlin edition in Russian reprinted in paperback: Ann Arbor, Ardis, 1976. ISBN 0-88233-25-2.

PG3476.N3W3
The Waltz Invention; a play in three acts. Translated from the Russian *Izobretenie Val'sa* by Dmitri Nabokov. New York, Phaedra, 1966, 111 p. Paperback by Pocket Books (75233), 1967. **891.7242.** 66-15639.

2. AUTOBIOGRAPHY

PG3476.N3Z52
Conclusive evidence, a memoir. New York, Harper & Bros., 1951, 240 p. **928.2** 51-9454.

> *"Unfortunately, the phrase* (Conclusive Evidence) *suggested a mystery story, and I planned to entitle the British edition* Speak, Mnemosyne *but was told that 'little old ladies would not want to ask for a book whose title they could not pronounce. I also toyed with* The Anthemian *which is the name of a honeysuckle ornament, consisting of elaborate interplacements and expanding clusters, but nobody liked it; so we finally settled for . . ."*

PG3476.N3Z5
Speak, memory; a memoir. London, Gollancz, 1951, 237 p., and New York, Grosset & Dunlap (The Universal library, UL-76), 1960, 240 p. First published under title: Conclusive Evidence. *(WARNING: This is NOT the version discussed in Parts 1-3.)* **928.2** 53-16547 and 60-2453.

PG3476.N3Z5/1966 & later dates
Speak, memory; an autobiography revisited, *rev. ed. (The version cited in Parts 1-3.)* New York, Putnam, 1966, and London, Weidenfeld & Nicolson, 1967, 316 p., illustrated. Paperbacks by Capricorn (329) and Penguin (2926). **818.5203.** 66-23330.

"*Its translations are . . .*

PG3476.N3Z517 (in Russian)
Drugie berega **(Other shores)**, translated by the author. New York, Chekohov Publishing House, 1954, 268 p., and Ann Arbor, Ardis, 1978, in cloth and paperback.
ISBN 0-88233-325-9. 55-23165.

"*. . . French, by Yvonne Davet* (Autres Rivages, *Gallimard, 1961), Italian, by Bruno Oddera* (Parla, Ricordo, *Mondadori, 1962), Spanish, by Jaime Pineiro Gonzáles* (¡Habla, memoria!, *1963) and German, by Dieter E. Zimmer (Rowohlt, 1964). This exhausts the necessary amount of bibliographic information, which jittery critics who were annoyed by the note at the end of* Nabokov's Dozen *will be, I hope, hypnotized into accepting at the beginning of the present work.*" —from Nabokov's foreword to the revised edition of *Speak, Memory* (1966).

3. ADDITIONAL

PS3527.A15635 (in French)
Olympia Press, *Paris*
L'affaire Lolita; défense de l'ecrivain. Paris, 1957, 105 p. *("The Lolita Affair: Defense of the Writer,"* in French. *Also see article in English,* "Lolita, *Nabokov, and I," by Maurice Girodias of Olympia Press,* Evergreen Review, *IX, Sep., 1965, pp. 44-47, 89-91, and Nabokov's rejoinder,* "Lolita and Mr. *Girodias,"* Evergreen Review, *XI, Feb., 1967, pp. 37-41)*

QL1.H3 vol. 101, no. 4
Nabokov, Vladimir Vladimirovich, 1899-1977
The nearctic members of the genus *Lycaeides Hübner* (Lycaenidae, Lepidoptera) Cambridge, MA, The Museum of Comparative Zoölogy at Harvard College, 1949. *Nabokov on butterflies:* pp. 479-541 of the Bulletin of the Museum of Comparative Zoology, with nine plates. **595.789** A 49-4134

4. TRANSLATIONS CRITICISM, LECTURES
(Alphabetically, by title)

"A book is assumed to be guilty until it presumes itself innocent — and not many do." — Norman Poshlost quoted in *The Beau and the Butterfly.*
ISBN 0-88233-658-4 (Russian only)

Alisa v Strane Chudes: Lewis Carroll's Alice in Wonderland as translated by Nabokov into Russian in 1923 in Berlin. Ann Arbor, Ardis. 1980, 114 p.

PG3347.E8N3
Eugene Onegin, a novel in verse by Aleksandr Pushkin (1799-1837). Translated from the Russian, with a commentary, by Vladimir Nabokov, 4 volumes. New York, Bollingen Foundation, distributed by Pantheon Books, 1964. Rev. ed. with Russian/English parallel text, Princeton, NJ, Princeton University Press, 1975, and London, Routledge and Kegan Paul, 1976.**891.7'1'3**. 70-38781 and 76-376222.

Hero of our time, by Mikhail Lermontov, translated by Vladimir and Dmitri Nabokov; New York, Doubleday, 1958.

Lectures on Literature by Vladimir Nabokov; edited by Fredson Bowers; introduction by John Updike. New York, Harcourt Brace Jovanovich and Columbia, SC, Bruccoli Clark, 1980, 385 p. *Nabokov on 19th and 20th century fiction.* Illustrated with reproductions of Nabokov's notes. 79-3690.

PG3012.N3
Lectures on Russian Literature by Vladimir Nabokov; edited, with an introduction, by Fredson Bowers. New York, Harcourt

Brace Jovanovich and Columbia SC, Bruccoli Clark, 1980, 324 p. *A companion volume: Nabokov on 19th-century fiction in his native land.* **891.7'09'003 19.** 81-47315.

PR6019.09U6844/1980 (Rare Bk Coll)
Lectures on Ulysses by Vladimir Nabokov, with a foreword by A. Walton Litz. Facsimile of the manuscript. Bloomfield Hills, Michigan, Bruccoli Clark, 1980, 144 p. *Nabokov on James Joyce.* "Five hundred copies have been printed, of which copies numbered 1 to 480 are for sale; copies i-xx are reserved for the publisher." **823'.912 19** 81-471133 r82.

PG3476.N3Z793
Nabokov's fifth arc: Nabokov and others on his life's work, edited by J. E. Rivers and Charles Nicol. Austin, University of Texas Press, 1982, 317 p. (The Dan Danciger publication series) **813'.54 19** 81-14764.

PG3476.N3Z787
Nabokov: the critical heritage, edited by Norman Page. London and Boston, Routledge & K. Paul, 1982. **813'.54 19** 82-3716.

PG3476.N3Z548
The Nabokov-Wilson letters: correspondence between Vladimir Nabokov and Edmund Wilson, 1940-1971; edited, annotated, and with an introductory essay by Simon Karlinsky. New York, Harper & Row, 1979, 346 p., includes bibliographic references and index. **813'.5'4 B.** 78-69627.

PG3335.N3
Nikolai Gogol, by Vladimir Nabokov. Norfolk CT, New Directions, 1944, 172 p. Later available in New Directions paperback (NDP78). London, Editions Poetry, 1947, and Weidenfeld & Nicolson, 1973. **891.73** 44-8135.

PG2531.I8N8
Notes on prosody from the commentary to his translation of Pushkin's Eugene Onegin by Vladimir Nabokov, New York, Bollingen Foundation, distributed by Pantheon Books, 1964, 104 p. Paperback by Princeton University Press. First published in 1964 as appendix two of the author's translation of Onegin. 64-23672.

PG3300.S6E57
The song of Igor's campaign; an epic of the twelfth century.
Translated from Old Russian by Vladimir Nabokov. New York, Random House, 1960, and London, Weidenfeld & Nicolson, 1961, 135 p. Later in Vintage Paperback (V718) and McGraw Hill hardcover (in 1975) and paperback (in 1981). Russian title: *Slovo o polku Igoreve*. 891.711 75-314894.

PS3527.A1557
Strong opinions, a collection of interviews, letters to editors, and articles. New York, McGraw-Hill, and London, Weidenfeld & Nicolson, 1973, 335 p. 818'.5'409. 75-301898.

PG3237.E5N3
Three Russian poets, selections from Pushkin, Lermontov and Tyutchev in new translations by Vladimir Nabokov. Norfolk CT, New Directions, 1944. 891.71082 45-35068.

"His translations, re-translations, pastiches, cross-linguistic imitations, etc., form a dizzying cat's cradle. No bibliographer has, until now, fully unraveled it. Nabokov has translated poems of Ronsard, Verlaine, Supervielle, Baudelaire, Musset, Rimbaud from French into Russian. Nabokov has translated the following English and Irish poets into Russian: Rupert Brooke, Seumas O'Sullivan Tennyson, Yeats, Byron, Keats, and Shakespeare. His Russian version of Alice in Wonderland (Berlin, 1923) has long been recognized as one of the keys to the whole Nabokov oeuvre ... Nabokov has published a Russian text of the Prologue to Goethe's Faust. One of his most bizarre feats is a re-translation back into English of Konstantin Bal'mont's ... Russian version of Edgar Allan Poe's The Bells."
— George Steiner in *TriQuarterly.*

**B.   ABOUT NABOKOV, VLADIMIR VLADIMIROVICH
(1899-1977)**
(Alphabetically, by author or editor)

"Nabokov, I have mastered your themes. (Nabokov, have I mastered your themes?) *See how your books lie carefully arranged in the window of my critical eye.* (I return your books, neatly packed and unsoiled, but I have kept and cut the pages and taken up the images.) *Each is an essential cubist plane of a bookish portrait that, in the necessary cultural perspective and light, is your truest and*

most palpable biography. (Together they form your future monument, the shadow of which even now extends from Moscow to New York.)" — Andrew Field in "In Place of a Foreword" to *Nabokov: His Life in Art.*

Appel, Alfred (ed.), **The Annotated Lolita** — See LOLITA in Section A.

PG3476.N3Z57
Appel, Alfred, Jr.
Nabokov's dark cinema. New York, Oxford University Press, 1974, 324 p., ill., **813'.5'4.** 74-79617.

PG3476.N3Z78 or PS3527.A15Z68
Appel, Alfred, Jr., and Newman, Charles (eds.)
TriQuarterly Festschrift:
Nabokov: criticism, reminiscences, translations, and tributes. Evanston, IL, Northwestern University Press, 1970, and London, Weidenfeld & Nicolson, 1971, 371 p., illus. (A TriQuarterly book) **813'.5'4.** 76-96906
(as a supplement to the above:)
PS3527.A15A8
Nabokov, Vladimir
Anniversary notes. Evanston, IL, Northwestern University Press, 1970, 15 p. **813'.5'4.** 71-26296.

PS3527.A15Z7
Bader, Julia
Crystal land: artifice in Nabokov's English novels. Berkeley, University of California Press. 1972, 162 p. 72-182277

PS3527.A15Z64
Bodenstein, Jurgen
The excitement of verbal adventure: a study of Vladimir Nabokov's English prose. Heidelberg, West Germany, university thesis. **813'.5'4.** 79-314841.

PR756.A987
Bruss, Elizabeth W.
Autobiographical acts: the changing situation of a literary genre. Baltimore, Johns Hopkins University Press, 1976, 184 p. *Deals with Nabokov's* Conclusive Evidence. **809.** 76-13460.

PS379.876
Bruss, Paul 1943-
Victims: textual strategies in recent American fiction. Lewisburg, PA, Bucknell University Press, and London, Associated University Presses, 1981, 259 p., incl. index and bibliography. *Deals with Nabokov, Donald Barthelme, and Jerzy Kosinski.* **813'.5'091.** 80-67319.

PS3527.A15Z66 (French)
Couturier, Maurice
Nabokov. Lausanne, Switzerland, L'Age d'homme, 1979, 173 p. (Cistre essai) **813'.54 19** 80-127401.

Z8608.6 F53
Field, Andrew, 1938-
Nabokov: a bibliography. New York, McGraw-Hill, 1973, 249 p. *Perhaps the most complete catalog of Nabokov's works up to that point. Includes his poetry, novels in Russian and English, chess problems, essays, studies of butterflies, interviews, and letters to editors.* 72-10473

PG3476.N3.Z64
Field, Andrew, 1938-
Nabokov, his life in art. Boston, Little, Brown, 1967, 397 p. **813'.5'4.** 67-14459.

PG3476.N3Z65
Field, Andrew, 1938-
Nabokov, his life in Part. New York, Viking, and London, Hamilton 1977, 285 p.; Penguin paperback, 1978, 299 p., illus. *"The book you hold does not come with the recommendation of Vladimir Nabokov."* **813'.5'4.** 76-47042 and 78-4075.

PS3527.A15Z7
Fowler, Douglas
Reading Nabokov. Ithaca, NY, Cornell University Press, 1974, 224 p., includes index and bibliography. **813'.5'4.** 73-20798.

PS3527.A15Z7213 (in English) and PS3527.A15Z72 (in German)
Grabes, Herbert
Fictitious biographies: Vladimir Nabokov's English novels.

The Hague, Mouton, 1977, 140 p. English translation of *Erfundene Biographien: Vladimir Nabokovs engl. Romane;* Tübingen, West Germany, Niemeyer, 1975, 130 p. **813'.5'4.** 77-564750 (English) and 76-464996 (German).

PG3476.N3Z67
Grayson, Jane
Nabokov translated: a comparison of Nabokov's Russian and English prose. Oxford, Oxford University Press, 1977, 257 p. **813'.5'4.** 77-358890.

PG3476.N3Z68
Hyde, George M.
Vladimir Nabokov: America's Russian novelist. London, M. Boyars, 1977, 230 p. (Critical appraisals series). Distributed in the U.S.A. by Humanities Press, Atlantic Highlands NJ. Includes index and bibliography. **813'.5'4.** 77-10462 and 78-307708.

PG3476.N327
Lee, Lawrence L.
Vladimir Nabokov. Boston, Twayne Publishers, 1976, 168 p. (Twayne's United States authors series) Includes index and bibliography. **813'.5'4.** 76-128.

PS3527.A15Z76
Lokrantz, Jessie Thomas
The underside of the weave: some stylistic devices used by Vladimir Nabokov. Uppsala, Sweden, Studia Anglististica Upsaliensia, Acta Universitatis Upsaliensis, 1973, 133 p. Thesis. **813'.5'4.** 74-150229.

PS3527.A15Z77
Maddox, Lucy
Nabokov's novels in English. Athens, University of Georgia Press, 1983. **813'.54 19** 82-4893.

PS3527.A15A6535
Mason, Bobbie Ann
Nabokov's garden: a guide to Ada. Ann Arbor, Ardis, 1975, 196 p., cloth and paperback editions. **813'.5'4.** 74-14070.

PG3476. N3Z69
McGraw, Harold, Jr., and others
In memoriam Vladimir Nabokov, 1899-1977. New York, McGraw-Hill, 1977, 42 p. Speeches made during a memorial service at the McGraw-Hill Book Store, New York, July 21, 1977. **813'.5'4B** 78-100995 r79.

PS3527.A15Z8
Morton, Donald E.
Vladmir Nabokov. New York, F. Ungar, 1974, 164 p. (Modern literature monographs) **813'.5'4.** 74-76128.

PG3476.N3Z75
Moynahan, Julius, 1925-
Vladimir Nabokov. Minneapolis, University of Minnesota Press, 1971, 47 p. (University of Minnesota pamphlets on American writers, no. 96) Includes bibliography. **813'.5'4.** 71-633325.

Nakhimovsky, A. D., and Paperno, V. A.: **An English-Russian Dictionary of Nabokov's Lolita** — See LOLITA in Section A.

PG3476.N3Z795/1978
Naumann, Marina Turkevich
Blue evenings in Berlin: Nabokov's short stories of the 1920s. New York, New York University Press, 1978, 254 p., includes index and bibliography. (New York University studies in comparative literature) **891.7'3'42.** 77-82751.

PS3527.A15Z86
Packman, David, 1949-
Vladimir Nabokov: the structure of literary desire. Columbia, University of Missouri Press, 1982. **813'.54 19** 82-70671.

PS228.M63P3
Paine, Sylvia, 1946-
Beckett, Nabokov, Nin: motives and modernism. Port Washington NY, Kennikat Press, 1981, 102 p. (Literary criticism series, National University Publications) *Deals with Samuel Beckett, 1906- , and Anais Nin, 1903-1977, as well as Nabokov.* **810'.9'005 19.** 81-5971.

PG3476.N3Z8
Pifer, Ellen
Nabokov and the novel. Cambridge MA, Harvard University Press, 1980, 97 p. Includes bibliographical references and index. **813'.54.** 80-16197.

PG3476.N3Z58
Proffer, Carl R. (ed.)
A Book of Things about Vladimir Nabokov. Ann Arbor, Ardis, 1974, 305 p., cloth and paperbound editions. **813'.5'4.** 75-306812.

PS3527.A15 L636
Proffer, Carl R.
Keys to Lolita. Bloomington, Indiana University Press, 1968, 160 p. 68-63001.

PG3476.N3Z93
Quennell, Peter, 1905-   (ed.)
Vladimir Nabokov, his life, his work, his world: a tribute. London, Weidenfeld & Nicolson, 1979, and New York, Morrow, 1980, 139 p. *Contents include Dmitri Nabokov's touching account of his father's last days, "On Revisiting Father's Room"; Alfred Appel's "Remembering Nabokov" through the years, and Hannah Green's* New Yorker *recollection of "Mr. Nabokov" as her teacher at Wellesley College.* Includes bibliography. **813'.54 B** 80-10081 and 80-451186.

Rivers, J.E., and Nicol, Charles (eds.), **Nabokov's Fifth Arc:** See Section A4 of this bibliography.

PS379.R73/1979
Rose-Werle, Kordula
Harlekinade: Genealogie u. Metamorphose: Struktur und Deutung d. Motivs bei J. D. Salinger u. V. Nabokov. (**Harlequinade: Genealogy and Metamorphosis: Structure and Meaning of Motifs in J.D. Salinger and V. Nabokov**) In German, with a summary in English. Frankfurt a.m., West Germany, Bern, Switzerland, and Cirencester, U.K.: Lang, 1979, 275 p. (Trier Studies in Literature) Originally presented as the author's thesis, University of Trier, West Germany. **813'.54'09351 19.** 80-497224.

PG3098.3.R68
Rowe, William Woodin
Nabokov & others: patterns in Russian literature. Ann Arbor, Ardis, 1979, 185 p., includes bibliographical references and index; cloth and paperbound editions. *". . . while over half of the book is devoted to Nabokov, other essays explore patterning in Pushkin, Lermontov, Gogol, and Dostoevsky."* **891.73'009.** 79-51639.

PG3476.N3Z84
Rowe, William Woodin
Nabokov's deceptive world. New York, New York University Press, 1971, 193 p., includes bibliographical references. **813'.5'4.** 76-158968.

PG3476.N3Z85
Rowe, William Woodin
Nabokov's Spectral Dimension: the other world in his works. Ann Arbor, Ardis, 1980, 186 p., includes bibliographic references. *"This book will change the way every lover of Nabokov's works reads and understands him."* **813'.54 19.** 80-29020.

Rowohlt Verlag GmbH
Vladimir Nabokov 1899-1977: Letters from Terra/Vladimir Nabokov zu Ehren (In Honor of Vladimir Nabokov). Reinbek bei Hamburg, West Germany, Rowohlt, 1977, 80 p. Tributes and memories printed for the friends of Nabokov and his German publisher. *Mostly in German, except for John Updike, "Transcending the Barriers of Language," and Heinrich Maria Ledig-Rowohlt, "Vevey 7.7.77," both in English.*

Z8608.6.534 or PG3476.N3
Schuman, Samuel
Vladimir Nabokov: a reference guide. Boston, G. K. Hall, 1979, 214 p. (A Reference publication in literature) **016.813'5'4.** 79-18355.

PG3476.N3Z86.
Shakovskaia, Zinaida (Princesse Zinaida Schakovsky, 1908-) *V poiskakh Nabokova.* Paris, La Presse Libre, 1979, 167 p., ill., includes bibliographic references. 80-511513.

Part of a 1965 national Educational Television (NET) interview with Nabokov was excerpted in the New York *Times* Sunday drama section, January 30, 1966, under the headline: "WHY NABOKOV DETESTS FREUD." In the TV interview, he also talked about *Ada* and "The Texture of Time."

Another BBC television interview, made during Nabokov's last months by Robert Robinson, appears in part as "The Last Interview" in Peter Quennell's anthology, *Vladimir Nabokov: His Life, His Work, His World: A Tribute* (see Section B).

5
CHRONOLOGY: TIME AND EBB*

1899   Born on April 22 (or April 23 or 10, depending on which calendar is used; see quote opening part 2) in St. Petersburg (now, Leningrad), to Vladimir Dmitrievich Nabokov, liberal jurist and politician, and the former Elena Ivanovna Rukavishnikov.

1900-1910   Educated by a succession of nannies, governesses, and tutors—largely British: *"I learned to read English before I could read Russian."* Boyhood in a St. Petersburg town house and country estate, Vyra, with a trip almost every year to southern France.

1911-1916   Attends St. Petersburg's most modern, liberal, progressive, private educational institute, the Tenishev School, where Vladimir Vladimirovich's daily arrival by auto, with liveried chauffeur doffing cap to young Master Nabokov, so disturbs the democratic eye of one teacher that he asks his pupil to please disembark two or three blocks from the school. In 1914, Nabokov composes his first poem and a verse brochure, containing a single poem of his with an epigraph from *Romeo and Juliet,* is privately printed.

1916   *Poems,* an edition of sixty-seven poems, is privately printed in Petrograd (as St. Petersburg was renamed in 1914). His Uncle Ruka (Vasiliy Ivanovich Rukavishnikov) dies, leaving his nephew a two thousand acre estate and "what would amount nowadays to a couple of million dollars."

1917-1918   As Russian Revolution begins, Nabokov's father serves briefly in Cabinet of A. F. Kerensky's provisional government (as executive secretary of Council of Ministers) and is elected to Constituent Assembly, but arrested by Bolshevik sailors when it is disbanded. Father escapes to Crimea and settles near Yalta with family.

---

*"Time and Ebb" is the title of a short story (1944) that foreshadows "The Texture of Time" in *Ada.* Primary sources for this chronology are *Speak, Memory,* Andrew Field's *Nabokov: His Life in Art,* and pp. xxxvii to xxxix of *Nabokov's Congeries,* edited by Page Stegner.

PN771.S74
Stark, John O.
The literature of exhaustion: Borges, Nabokov, and Barth.
Durham, NC, Duke University Press, 1974, 196 p., includes bibliography and index. *Deals with Jorge Luis Borges and John Barth as well as Nabokov.* **813'.5'409.** 73-92536.

PS3527.A15Z85 or PG3476.N3Z87
Stegner, Page
Escape into aesthetics; the art of Vladimir Nabokov. New York, Dial Press, 1966, and London, Eyre & Spottiswoode, 1967, 141 p., includes bibliography. **818.5408** 66-22588.

PG3476.N3Z89
Stuart, Dabney, 1937-
Nabokov: the dimensions of parody. Baton Rouge, Louisiana State University Press, 1978, 191 p., includes bibliographic references. **813'.5'4.** 77-20870.

Paris Review Interview: "Vladimir Nabokov," by Herbert Gold in *Paris Review* No. 41, summer-fall, 1967, pp. 92-111. Gold also wrote "Artist in Pursuit of Butterflies" in *Saturday Evening Post*, February 11, 1957, pp. 81-85.

Playboy Interview: "Vladimir Nabokov," by Alvin Toffler in January, 1964 *Playboy*, pp. 35-45. Reprinted in *The Twelfth Anniversary Playboy Reader* (Playboy Press, 1965); *Playboy Interviews* (Playboy Press, 1967), and *The Playboy Interview* (Wideview Books, 1981).

Russian Literature Triquarterly (RLT) devoted its third issue (Spring, 1972) to Romanticism and Nabokov. Articles included: Larry Gregg, *"Slava Snabokovu";* Ludmila A. Foster, "Nabokov in Russian Emigre Criticism"; Anthony Olcott, "The Author's Special Intention: A Study of *The Real Life of Sebastian Knight*"; Paul Grams, *"Pnin:* the Biographer as Meddler"; Kevin Pilon, "A Chronology of *Pale Fire*"; D. Barton Johnson, "Synthesia, Polychromatism, and Nabokov," and Carl R. Proffer, *"Ada* as Wonderland." The issue, unfortunately, is out-of-print at its source —Ardis Publishers, 2901 Heatherway, Ann Arbor, Michigan

48104 — but the address is worth retaining, as Ardis is the prime source (virtually the ONLY source) of Nabokov in Russian and, as this bibliography indicates, a major purveyor of Nabokov accessories in English, too.

Time cover story on "Vladimir Nabokov: The Novel is Alive and Living in Antiterra" ("Prospero's Progress"), May 23, 1969.

Curley, Dorothy Nyren, and Maurice and Elaine Fialka Kramer: MODERN AMERICAN LITERATURE: A Library of Literary Criticism, Fourth Enlarged Edition, Volume II (G-O), has an excellent section on Nabokov, pp. 395-402. New York, Frederick Ungar Co., 1969.

C. AUDIO-VISUAL & MISCELLANY

Lolita and Poems: Vladimir Nabokov, read by Vladimir Nabokov, on Spoken Arts LP record 902. Side 1 is from chapter 35 of *Lolita* (the death of Quilty). Side 2 is seven poems: "The Ballad of Longwood Glen," "Rain," "Lines Written in Oregon," "On Translating Eugene Onegin," "An Evening of Russian Poetry," "The Swift," and "The Discovery."

Lolita (1962), a film directed by Stanley Kubrick and produced by James B. Harris. Script by Vladimir Nabokov based on his own novel. Cast headed by James Mason as Humbert, Sue Lyon as Lolita, Shelley Winters as Charlotte Haze, and Peter Sellers as Clare Quilty. Released by Metro-Goldwyn-Mayer. Running time: 153 minites.

King Queen Knave (1972), a German-American co-production (also called *Herzbube*) by Jerzy Skolimowski starring David Niven, Gina Lollobrigida, and John Moulder Brown.

A 1962 British Broadcasting Corporation (BBC) television interview with Nabokov by Peter Duval Smith was printed in *The Listener* (November 22, 1962, pp. 856-858) and reprinted in the U.S. by Vogue (March 1, 1963, pp. 152-155).

1918-1919   *Two Paths,* an almanac of twenty poems, twelve by V. V. Nabokov, is published in Petrograd. In between two Bolshevik occupations, Nabokov's father serves as minister of justice ("of minimal justice," he puts it wryly) in the Crimean regional government. *"In March of 1919, the Reds broke through in northern Crimea, and from various ports a tumultuous evacuation of anti-Bolshevik groups began. Over a glassy sea in the bay of Sebastopol, under wild machine-gun fire from the shore (the Bolshevik troops had just taken the port), my family and I set out for Constantinople and Piraeus on a small and shoddy Greek ship Nadezhda (hope) carrying a cargo of dried fruit."* The Nabokovs leave Greece on *May 18, 1919,* on the Cunard liner *Pannonia,* bound for New York *("twenty-one years too soon as far as I was concerned"),* but they disembark in Marseilles and move on to London. After "several expensive months in a rented house in Elm Park Gardens," paid for by what little jewelry Nabokov's mother salvaged in their escape, his father moves to Berlin to edit emigré newspaper, *The Rudder,* taking wife and three youngest children (Olga, b. 1903; Elena, b. 1906; Kirill, b. 1911) and sending the two oldest sons to Cambridge: Sergey (b. 1900) to Christ College and Vladimir to Trinity College.

1919-1923   Studies French and Russian literature at Cambridge *("The story of my college years in England is really the story of my trying to become a Russian writer.")*

1922   Translates Rupert Brooke's poems and Roman Rulland's *Colas Breugnon* into Russian and is graduated with honors. On *March 28, 1922,* while Vladimir Vladimirovich visits his family in Berlin, his father, Vladimir Dmitrievich, is assassinated there *"by a sinister ruffian whom, during World War Two, Hitler made administrator of emigre Russian affairs."* In 1923 in Berlin, Nabokov (as "V. Sirin") publishes two poetry collections in Russian: *"The Empyrean Path* and *The Cluster;* the former is dedicated *"To the Memory of My Father."* He also translates *Alice in Wonderland* into Russian for $5. *May, 1923:* Meets

	Véra Evseevna Slonim, daughter of a Russian industrialist also ruined by the Revolution.
1923-1937	Resident alien in Berlin: stateless person with Nansen passport. Prodigious contributor of fiction, poetry, reviews, and chess problems to émigré publications under Sirin pseudonym.
1924	Petrograd is renamed Leningrad.
1925	*April 15:* Marries Véra Slonim. Starts work on *Mary*.
1926	*Mary* is published in Russian by Slovo, Berlin, and goes generally unnoticed.
1927	*King Queen Knave* is "conceived on the coastal sands of Pomerania Bay."
1928	*KQKn* is completed in summer and published in October by Slovo; *Mary* is published in German translation by Ullstein, Berlin. Ullstein also acquires German rights to *KQKn* for translation by Siegfreid von Vegesack.
1929	Nabokov uses Ullstein's "generous advance" for a "butterfly safari" in the Pyrenees Orientales, where, at the spa of Le Boulou, he begins writing *The Defense*.
1930	*The Defense* is published in Russian by Slovo as *The Luzhin Defense*. *The Eye* is serialized in Russian in *Contemporary Annals,* and *The Return of Chorb* is published in Russian in Berlin. At this point, says Andrew Field, Sirin "now begins to be widely written about and discussed as the most important of the younger emigre writers. At no time during his émigré writing career, however, did Nabokov's books ever produce more than a few hundred dollars a year. Nabokov earned his living by giving lessons in tennis, English, and Russian."

1932	Fifth novel, *Glory,* published in Russian in Paris. Sixth novel, *Kamera obskura* (later *Laughter in the Dark*), published in Russian in Paris and Berlin. Begins work on *Despair.*
1934	*May:* Nabokov's only child, Dmitri Vladimirovich, born in Berlin, Nazi Germany. *Despair* is serialized in Russian in Paris and the influential critic Vladislav Khodasevich hails it with these words; "*The Luzhin Defense* is the best thing written by Sirin, and *Despair* is not inferior to it." With *Despair,* a few émigré readers and writers begin to mention Sirin in the same breath as the great figures of Russian literature.
1935	*Invitation to a Beheading* is serialized in Russian; the switch into allegory generates some controversy among Sirin's readers. He begins writing *The Gift.*
1936	*Despair* is published in book form in Russian and Nabokov undertakes its English translation. *Kamera Obskura* is published in English translation as *Camera Obscura.*
1937	John Long, Ltd., London, publishes *Despair* in English, with ads for their other publications at the end: "*Despite that bonus, the book sold badly, and a few years later a German bomb destroyed the entire stock.*" The Nabokovs move from "Hitler's Germany" to "Maginot's France," settling in Paris (1937-40) where Nabokov does some of his writing in English and French. *The Gift* is finished on the French Riviera and serialized in Russian in Paris, but his editors reject chapter 4.
1938	Nabokov publishes two plays in Russian: *The Event* and *The Waltz Invention. The Event* is produced by the Russian Theater in Paris. *Invitation to a Beheading* is published as a book in Russian in Paris. *Camera Obscura* becomes *Laughter in the Dark* in American version revised by Nabokov.

1939	*Despair* is published in French (as *La Méprise*) by Gallimard (translated from Nabokov's English translation) and panned by what Nabokov calls "a Communist reviewer (J. P. Sartre)."
1940	*Solux Rex*, forerunner of *Pale Fire* (1962) begins running serially in Russian in Paris, but it and its periodical are aborted by the fall of France to Hitler. Nabokov seeks academic post in England, but is unsuccessful. *May:* the Nabokovs leave France, sailing on the liner *Champlain* to New York. Lectures on Slavic languages at Stanford University.
1941-1948	Lecturer (generally thrice weekly) at Wellesley loosely attached to six departments: English Composition, English Literature, French, German, Spanish, and Italian.
1942-1948	Research Fellow in Entomology, Museum of Comparative Zoology at Harvard, while lecturing at Wellesley.
1941	*The Real Life of Sebastian Knight*, written in English in Paris, is published by New Directions.
1942	Association with *The New Yorker* (he acknowledges, *"through Edmund Wilson"*) begins with publication of a short poem.
1943	Awarded first Guggenheim Fellowship "to assist research and artistic creation."
1944	New Directions publishes his books, *Nikolai Gogol*, in Makers of Modern Literature series, and *Three Russian Poets: Selections from Pushkin, Lermontov and Tyurchev in New Translations*.
1945	Naturalized as American citizen.
1947	*Bend Sinister* is published by Henry Holt, New York, and *Nine Stories* (four of them translated from Russian) by New Directions.

1948-1959	Professor of Russian and European literature at Cornell University, during which stint he writes his autobiography as well as *Lolita, Pnin,* and his translations of *The Song of Igor's Campaign* and *Eugene Onegin* with massive commentaries, stories, and poems, and articles on lepidoptera.
1951	*Conclusive Evidence* (later, *Speak, Memory*) is published by Harper Bros., New York.
1951-1952	Guest lecturer at Harvard.
1952	Makes a "readable translation" for teaching purposes of *The Song of Igor's Campaign.* This version (called *The Discourse of Igor's Campaign*) of the twelfth-century epic is discarded in favor of his more restrained and scholarly 1960 translation. *Fifteen Poems 1929-1951* published in full *in Russian* by Chekhov Publishing House, New York.
1953	Awarded second Guggenheim Fellowship. Awarded $1,000 by American Academy of Arts and Letters. His translation of his autobiography is published in Russian by "that Samaritan organization," Chekhov of New York as *Other Shores.*
1955	*Lolita* is published in Paris by Olympia Press.
1956	Graham Greene, in England, recommends *Lolita* as one of the best books of 1955, causing controversy in British press that spreads to New York *Times Book Review.* Meanwhile, Nabokov (according to Andrew Field) is proposed for an important chair at a "Great University" in England, but the motion is defeated with this comment: "Gentlemen, even if one allows that he is an important writer, are we next to invite an elephant to be Professor of Zoology?" Chekhov of New York publishes *Spring in Fialta and Other Stories* in Russian.
1957	*The Anchor Review* (no. 2, 1957) devotes 112 pages to

	Nabokov and excerpts from *Lolita*. *Pnin* is published by Doubleday.
1958	*Lolita* is published by G. P. Putnam's Sons and becomes a best-seller. *Nabokov's Dozen* (thirteen short stories) and his co-translation (with son Dmitri) of Lermontov's *A Hero of Our Time* are both published by Doubleday.
1959	*Invitation to a Beheading* published in English by Putnam. Doubleday publishes his *Poems*. *Lolita* is sold to movies (for a reported $150,000) and Nabokov can afford to resign from Cornell and devote his entire working time to writing: "I never imagined that I should be able to live by my writing, but now I am kept by a little girl named *Lolita*."
1960	He works on *Lolita* screenplay for Stanley Kubrick. Mr. and Mrs. Nabokov move to Switzerland to be near Dmitri, who is pursuing an opera career in Italy. Nabokov's *Song of Igor's Campaign* translation is published by Random House.
1962	*Pale Fire* is published by Putnam. Nabokov attends premiere of *Lolita* and goes unrecognized while celebrity-watching announcer hails the entrance of columnist Louis Sobol.
1963	*The Gift* is published in English by Putnam.
1964	*Eugene Onegin* translation and commentaries is published in four volumes by Bollingen Foundation and controversy with Edmund Wilson and others goes on for two years. *The Defense* is published in English by Putnam.
1965	*The Eye* is published in English by Phaedra, Inc., New York.
1966	*Despair* and the revised, expanded, definitive *Speak, Memory* autobiography are published by Putnam;

	The Waltz Invention (play) and *Nabokov's Quartet*, (short stories) by Phaedra. *Invitation to a Beheading* is reprinted in Russian in Paris. Page Stegner's *Escape into Aesthetics: The Art of Vladimir Nabokov* is published by Dial Press, New York.
1967	Phaedra publishes Nabokov's translation of *Lolita* into Russian and Nabokov switches his principal New York publishing affiliation from Putnam to McGraw-Hill. Andrew Field's *Nabokov: His Life in Art* is published by Little, Brown & Co., Boston.
1968	*King Queen Knave* comes out in English under McGraw-Hill imprint. Viking publishes *Nabokov's Congeries* (Page Stegner, ed.), and Indiana University Press publishes *Keys to Lolita* by Carl R. Proffer.
1969	*Ada*, first new novel in seven years, is published by McGraw-Hill, which also issues Russian facsimile edition of *King Queen Knave*. Nabokov celebrates seventieth birthday in April and, on *May 23*, he adorns the cover of *Time*.
1970	His first novel, *Mary*, appears in English, and the injection of Alfred Appel, Jr., into his best-known breeds *The Annotated Lolita;* both books from McGraw-Hill. *TriQuarterly* devotes its winter issue to honoring Nabokov at seventy.
1971	*Poems and Problems*, including eighteen chess problems, and *Glory* are issued by McGraw-Hill. The latter completes the cycle of Nabokov's nine Russian novels. *October 31:* "Understanding Vladimir Nabokov: A Red Autumn Leaf Is a Red Autumn Leaf, Not a Deflowered Nymphet" appears in the New York *Times Magazine*.
1972	*Glory* is the January selection of the Book-of-the-Month Club. *Transparent Things*, first new novel since *Ada*, is published by McGraw-Hill and is the July Book Find Club selection.

1973	*A Russian Beauty and Other Stories* is published by McGraw-Hill.
1974	Latest novel, *Look at the Harlequins!* is selected by Literary Guild. *April:* Celebrates seventy-fifth birthday in Montreux whole son Dmitri accepts National Medal of Literature (a bronze medallion and $10,000 given annually by the National Book Committee to "a living American writer for the excellence of his or her total contribution to the world of letters") on Vladimir Nabokov's behalf in ceremony at New York Public Library.
1975	*Tyrants Destroyed, and Other Stories* published.
1976	*Details of a Sunset and Other Stories* and revised translation of *Eugene Onegin* published.
1977	Andrew Field's *Nabokov: His Life in Part* is published. Richard Locke, an editor of The New York Times Book Review, writes that the currently preeminent American novelists are Vladimir Nabokov, Saul Bellow, Norman Mailer, John Updike, and Thomas Pynchon. *July 2, 1977:* Death in Montreux.